Confident Music Performance

Fix the Fear of Facing an Audience

Ruth Bonetti

Other books by Ruth Bonetti

Taking Centre-Stage

Practice is a Dirty Word

Don't Freak Out – Speak Out

Enjoy Playing the Clarinet

Confident Music Performance
© Ruth Bonetti 2003

Published by :
Words and Music
PO Box 422,
The Gap Qld 4061 Australia
Phone (+61) 07 3300 2286
Mobile (+61) 0411 782 404
http://www.ruthbonetti.com

Second edition, 2006

National Library of Australia
Cataloguing-in-Publication data:

Bonetti, Ruth
Confident Music Performance

ISBN 0 9578861 6 0

1. Music – Performance –
Psychological aspects.
2. Stage fright. I. Title.

780.78

Cover design: Peter Fenoglio
Illustrations: Peter Fenoglio
Pre-Press: Bob Johnson

Originally published in 1997 by Albatross Books Pty Ltd Sydney, Australia under the title *Taking Centre-Stage*.

Contents

Introduction

'YOU CANNOT BE A MUSICIAN without living with the hobgoblins and demons of insecurity,' advises Lynn Harrell, the American cellist and director of the Royal Academy of Music, London. 'As you go through your career, have the courage to know that they are there … If you feel the raucous cackle of the crowd pushing in on you, then push it back and away and make the space in which to remember why you became a musician in the first place.

'Music is about man's deepest feelings and aspirations. The irony is that as we get older we get more and more embarrassed about expressing that … Don't be afraid of the nakedness – without it there is no expression.'

What a career hazard!

Most performers have been inhibited by nerves at some time or another; many top musicians have been paralysed by them at times, yet their creativity and reputation triumphed. Johannes Brahms was too inhibited to play before Franz Liszt; Ludwig van Beethoven despaired after a public fiasco; the wunderkind Felix Mendelssohn fled the room in tears when performing for Hummel.

Highly creative, sensitive performers often suffer the most from nerves, while matter-of-fact people may cope better. The very sensitivity that enriches exceptional performances often works against the artists instead of for them. Some of the greatest talents never realise their full potential because of nerves. Their vivid imaginations, capable of drawing out the sublime, can also predict numerous mishaps and stumbles, turning the minutes, hours, days or weeks before a performance into miseries of imaginings, many unlikely to eventuate.

We performers face exposure of vulnerable weaknesses, lack of ability, preparation or poise. Defensive thoughts swirl through our minds: all those upraised eyes are aimed at me. Surely my quivering knees and fingers are obvious. Trapped up here under these glaring,

1

hot footlights, both physically and emotionally 'fight-or-flight' are denied me. I am alienated, alone and exposed up on the bare boards of the stage, on trial, confronting my peers who sit cushioned in group anonymity.

I am afraid that people will discover just how little work I did. What will they think of me? My self-esteem has plummeted, for it seems my worth as a person hangs on that frayed thread of the brilliance of my presentation. A telescopic lens magnifies mistakes in my mind. The footlights' laser beam impresses those mistakes indelibly in my memory.

To all of you who suffer from such agonies I say, take heart. You suffer because you are not a potato. Does a potato possess your abilities, your sensitivity or richness of imagination? Do you want to play like a potato? Do people pay to hear potatoes perform? Your creativity makes life harder, but it sets you apart.

The purpose of this book is to help you turn those negatives which may block you into positives which can allow your talent to blossom, your soul to soar. It will help you understand and anticipate, utilise and even welcome that rush of adrenaline which, when excessive, causes panic. However, when properly channelled, this adrenaline can lift a performance from the merely mundane to an exciting, enriching and communicating event. In this way performance tension is changed into vital energy.

As I listened to a talk on performance anxiety given by a psychiatrist at a music conference, I realised the need for a practical book to help people cope with their nerves. It seemed obvious from the listeners' avid response and eager questions that many sought help for their anxiety and wanted to learn ways to a better performance. I found the scientific-medical aspect of the talk interesting, but related best to the few personal moments when the speaker discussed how he had faced his own nerves prior to the lecture. However, I was concerned that his main solution was medication: 'beta blockers'. Surely there must be more natural, practical solutions?

I thought back to my own concerto performance a few days before and the props I had used to steel myself. A colleague had shared the backstage warm-up room, and out of the corner of my eye I noticed with interest her routine of preparation and relaxation. Did my own elaborate procedures help? Yes, to a large extent. Yet it was my attitude of mind that most influenced the outcome of the performance.

Ironically, even though I knew I could play a work that I had performed many times before, I was inhibited by wondering if the 'heavies' of the profession were in the hall ... only to discover later that they weren't! I realised how often our communication with the audience is inhibited by such misconceptions.

Often we imagine criticism where none is intended. Even if it were, is it not better to play for ourselves and for the appreciative, rather than for those few who make an art-form of criticising? Often the loudest, most derisive voices belong to defensive, insecure rivals who try to make themselves bigger by knocking us down to size.

Soon after this concert, I spent a week travelling in country areas to examine music candidates. Every day I encountered several candidates, usually well motivated adults, whose nerves reduced them to quivering jelly. It was obvious they were keen and had prepared diligently. In spite of my tight schedule, I felt compelled to take time to help them cope with their nerves. This book was conceived during my return flight as I thought over their problems and how I'd handled similar situations. Since we all experience our careers and communications differently I knew that my one voice could not find answers to such varied problems. We all tread our paths differently. I decided to offer a holistic approach, a smorgasbord of suggestions from which readers could nibble at will, according to their taste or need.

Performance encompasses the whole person, so it is necessary to offer a wide range of solutions – physical, mental, emotional and spiritual. All the people who populate this book are its life-blood. Whether a 'big-name' or a suburban music teacher, they are real people, triumphing over real dragons. These flesh and blood and heart people, who may have risked vulnerability by being quoted, have courageously and openly shared their experiences in order to help others. I hope that the performing arts scene may seem a more understanding place as a result.

If others' ideas have not been credited, this is because in the weft

3

and warp of experience, one absorbs many ideas without knowing or remembering their source. Many are passed on by our modern version of folklore, teaching. I thank all those who have in many ways given insight, contributions, feedback, encouragement and support, who read or edited chapters.

Thank you, especially, to my husband, Antoni, who has been a constant sounding-board, for making suggestions from his own expertise as a violinist, conductor and educator, for his endurance through countless rewrites and for sharing with me so many enriching musical adventures.

The following chapters will fortify those facing public performance as well as their teachers and parents. This book seeks to encourage and empower all who communicate from centre-stage.

Part A

The Problem

The fear and reward we share

*I was kind of nervous. It wasn't stage fright – it was a
thing called death! I would stand in the wings and my
whole life would pass before my eyes.*
— Actor/singer Barbra Streisand

IS THIS YOUR EXPERIENCE? We sailed through the last rehearsal
before the performance. Overall we have prepared pretty well,
working frantically hard the last few days!

But when we walk on stage, suddenly we feel exposed. All those
eyes bore into us, our weaknesses seem pitifully obvious. Once we
stumble over that first wobbly note, all confidence shrivels up. We
keep peering back to that mistake, as much use as continually
touching a sore tooth.

From then on we skid downhill as more notes topple, ricochet. Our
fingers tangle like spaghetti; we are tongue-tied. Dry-mouthed, we
feel confused and inhibited. We sense the people nearby sprouting
huge bulbous ears like the old His Master's Voice gramophone
trumpet, into which our pitiful sounds drip.

The piece falls apart, the rhythm muddles and expressive flow
dries up in a sludgy quagmire. Out of a mind as blank as a crashed
computer screen, our only thought is a plaintive refrain: 'How could
this be happening to me? I played it perfectly this morning!'

Sounds familiar? Of course, we imagine the fiasco is ours alone.
But many other performers have felt such horrors. Stage fright is no
respecter of persons. Anyone may experience it at some time in their
career. It is not a personality trait or mental disorder, but a response to

a certain pressured situation. The secret is to learn from experienced players how to channel the adrenaline and turn it to positive use.

Famous performers face and conquer nerves daily

Our role models seem to inhabit a loftier stratum. We pit ourselves against the perfection of recording technicians who can aid those performers by snippetting in correct notes and adjusting tuning with the turn of a dial. Many top performers suffer agonies of nerves because tonight's audience expects the perfection of recordings that were produced through days of retakes.

It may be comforting to know that the famous performers we try to emulate suffer as we do, some of them excruciatingly, for they have high reputations at stake. The Italian tenor Luciano Pavarotti writes:

> *Friends often say to me when they see me suffering before a performance, 'How can you be nervous? You are Pavarotti, the world-famous tenor!' They don't understand that the reputation can make it worse. Being famous ... doesn't turn you into a supernatural being. You are still a mortal man who can catch a sore throat, be out of form or make a mistake. All the fame and talk of number one adds to the pressure, but not to your excellence.*
>
> *If anything, that [pressure] stimulated me more than depressed me. If at the beginning I hadn't learned to control my nerves, just as I had learned to control my breathing and diaphragm support, I would have given up my career years ago.*
>
> (My Own Story, Luciano Pavarotti, pp. 275-6)

Cellist Pablo Casals, pianist Vladimir Horowitz, Russian pianist Josef Lhevinne and composer/pianist Ignacy Paderewski, among others, have had to be pushed on stage. Once there, they played brilliantly. Anton Rubenstein had a brilliant career as a pianist but, when his memory became unreliable around the age of fifty, he described his reactions:

> *Since then I have been conscious of a growing weakness. I begin to feel an uncertainty: something like a nervous dread often takes possession of me while I am on stage in the presence of a large audience ... This sense of uncertainty has often inflicted on me*

tortures only to be compared with those of the Inquisition, while
the public listening to me imagines that I am perfectly calm.

(*Success in Music and How It is Won*, Henry F. Fink, p. 305)

Though these horrors did not deter them, both Rubenstein and Horowitz later admitted they were still getting butterflies before every concert. The perfectionist Jascha Heifitz strove for impeccable violin technique as a bulwark against nerves. Pablo Casals spoke of his dreadful feeling of nervousness before a performance: 'It is always an ordeal. Before I go on stage, I have a pain in my chest. I'm tormented. The thought of a public performance is still a nightmare.' (*Joys and Sorrows – Pablo Casals*, Albert E. Kahn, p. 46)

These anecdotes give numerous examples of the nerves experienced by performers of all levels and in all performing art forms. I hope these examples will encourage players struggling with nerves to realise that:

The degree of performance anxiety experienced is not related to the level of the player's talent … or lack of it. Some excitement is natural when on stage, otherwise we should not be there! Many mistake normal excitement for nerves. There are many ways that players can learn to cope with nerves, even turn them to positive advantage. Without some charge of that potent electricity, adrenaline, a performance would be matter-of-fact, complacent and boring.

Most top performers live with nerves and successfully combat them regularly. Yet many sufferers of stage fright nurse their nerves as an embarrassing dark secret, rather like incontinence, imagining they are the only ones to experience them.

Given that nerves are a problem, why perform?

Aged ninety, Pablo Casals told why, during a long, intensive performing life, he endured such agonies:

I, for one, cannot dream of retiring. Not now or ever. I don't
believe in retirement for anyone in my type of work, not while the
spirit remains. My work is my life. I cannot think of one without
the other … The man who works and is never bored is never old.
Work and interest in worthwhile things are the best remedy for old
age. Each day I am reborn. Each day I must begin again.

(*Joys and Sorrows – Pablo Casals*, Albert E. Kahn, pp. 16-17)

8

After the effort of preparation and stoking ourselves up, the resulting 'high' of achievement, of conquering the Everest of our fears, is addictive. It is an exciting life, with less of the humdrum routine which depresses many other workers. Sooner or later there is some reward of appreciation. The experience of communicating to an audience, and feeling and hearing their response, is a heady one. After a few successful experiences, it is in our blood.

Sydney singer Grahame McIntosh sums it up:

Most opera companies send a letter detailing the role and dates about two months before each season begins. An Italian tenor told me: 'You know soma people geta de nerves befora they go on stage. Me, I geta de nerves when I geta da letter.'

Each time we arrived in the wings, a famous Welsh soprano would say to me, 'Grahame, what are we doing here?' I would reply: 'Because the theatre is in our blood and we couldn't bear to do anything else.'

We put ourselves through agonies of preparation and performance because we have heard music or words so beautiful, so powerful, so moving that they warmed our souls. We long to be a part of that, to capture and cherish that memory, to hold it longer by experiencing its depths.

We perform because it is rewarding to give out to others, to give them pleasure, as Gerald Moore writes:

I revel in the sensation of getting hold of my listeners, riveting their attention, communicating ideas to them, making them smile. When an audience is responsive and lively, I am conscious of a wave of goodwill which flows from it and gives me strength and confidence.

(*Am I Too Loud?* Gerald Moore, p.235)

We do it because we want to communicate to the audience. Guitarist Julian Bream writes:

What I do know is that I've got something to communicate, something to give and, however modest it is, give it I must. I might even call it a duty. I want to say something to other people. A gentle and tiny utterance it may be, but I believe it can also be on occasions compelling and beautiful. Also, there are all those really promising young guitar players around now and, just as I

remember when I was a young boy, I learned such a lot from
hearing and watching Segovia at his recitals, so I believe that
many of the younger generation of budding recitalists may be able
to pick up quite a bit one way or another from my efforts on the
concert platform.

(*A Life on the Road*, Julian Bream, p. 34)

But most excitingly, we do it because of those memorable performances which flowed smoothly, when our spirits reached out to the audience and we sensed their response. The indescribable experience of reaching complete strangers with the beauty and expression of our music, speech or movement is exciting and moving. We are humbled to be part of the deeper mysteries of communication, where our spirit meets those of others.

Pianist Lili Kraus:

It was Goethe, I think, who said, 'The hallmark of genius is love'.
If you don't have that love in you, how can you express it? ... I
think that when an audience is thrilled for technical reasons, this
thrill is on the surface. When listeners are moved because they
have received the performer's emotional message, this is both
elating and lasting.

(*Pianists at Play*, Dean Elder, p. 68.)

My husband and I experienced this after a concert we gave in Sweden. An acquaintance, Agneta, with whom our communication had been previously superficial due to our respective language limitations, hugged us and asked with tears in her eyes: 'What is it that you have? I felt your spirit, God's spirit, tonight.' Memories of stress, tension and nerves quickly fade before such words.

Summary

- **We are not alone! Most performers experience some degree of nerves, which has no relation to lack of talent. In fact, many famous performers have struggled nightly with 'butterflies' – yet triumphed.**
- **We perform because it can be so rewarding, despite the problems and symptoms of fear.**

2

Symptoms of fear and why we feel afraid

To be shot at dawn, or stage fright. Which would you prefer? I think that many stage fright sufferers might prefer the former. To stand behind the curtain and hear the low growl of an audience, gradually growing in size, is a unique experience. At this point, if someone opened the stage door, you could beat the four-minute mile home, no matter how many miles.

Sydney singer Grahame McIntosh

FEAR IS A REASONABLE, SENSIBLE EMOTION which causes us to protect ourselves from catastrophe or problems. A degree of fear is useful; it motivates us to take precautions and even lifesaving actions. If we fear an armed robber, we can take sensible precautions like double-locked doors and burglar alarms to ensure better sleep. Similarly, if we dread that a difficult passage of semiquavers will fall apart in performance, we should practise it every day, starting well beforehand.

If I need to run from a dangerous situation, fear may cause me to find amazing resources of strength I never thought possible. During a performance, healthy fear (of losing a job or being downgraded) may sharpen my concentration, increase my energy and endurance, and clarify my thoughts. It may also intensify my imagination, so that after a lacklustre rehearsal, I find myself inflecting new subtlety and depth of feelings into the performance. A reasonable degree of fear is valid, even useful.

Extremes manifest as panic (a sudden surge of acute fear) and irrational anxiety, when we act as if we are under great stress, although there may be no apparent cause. Discuss these with a counsellor or teacher. The ensuing chapters offer suggestions such as breathing and relaxation techniques to help combat such fears.

Many performers have experienced sensations reflecting their performance anxiety such as:

- **dry mouth, or flowing gushes of saliva**
- **shallow breathing, resulting in shaky, vibratoed sound from singers, wind and brass players**
- **the fear of not having enough air to get through the phrase**
- **breath-holding, often unconsciously, robbing the body of vital oxygen**
- **panic-rushing of rhythm and pace, losing clarity of articulation; shaky hands, knees, mouth**
- **neck muscles tightening and pulling the head down and shoulders up**
- **lack of control**
- **memory blanks**

Standing performers have to cope with quivering knees that threaten to buckle under them. They may unconsciously lock their knees to counteract this, which only transmits excess tension through the whole body.

String musicians struggle to control a wobbly bow, afraid of dropping the violin altogether. Some orchestral players seated on the edge of the stage fear falling off into the laps of a bemused audience. Fingers shake, sometimes uncontrollably, slipping off the keys, fingerboard or keyboard.

As well as 'on the night' symptoms, tension escalates through the days and nights before the event. This may induce nightmares, lack of sleep, or fitful, restless dozing, irritability, the inability to concentrate. And then, just before the performance, a queasy stomach, diarrhoea, fidgets and shaky hands may threaten our already fragile poise as the dreaded moment comes closer and closer.

Why we have these symptoms of fear

Why do these symptoms occur? If we take a look at how our body reacts physiologically when we are under stress the answer is simple.

All these symptoms are part of the 'fight or flight' reaction. In fact, within a matter of seconds over one thousand changes mobilise the body for action. These physiological changes are positive and designed to protect us. Unfortunately, such reactions sometimes seem overwhelming, to be working against us instead of for us. Consequently we may blame ourselves for 'faults and failures', thinking 'There's something wrong with me'. These reactions are part and parcel of the adrenaline rush.

At the mere thought of a threatening situation, our body prepares for fight or flight. The symptoms of this response include:

- **Increase in heart rate and our blood pressure.**
- **More blood pumps to our brain, maximising clarity of thought, and to our muscles to prepare for action.**
- **Simultaneously, blood is pumped away from the digestive system to conserve energy.**

These normal, built-in reactions provide us with a defence mechanism to cope with short-term stress situations. Ironically, these protective, positive reactions often hinder us from keeping a clear head, a calm poise and an ability to project during a performance. In fact, stage fright mimics those reactions that occur automatically in any stressful situation.

Like pianist Claudio Arrau, we can learn to channel the positive reactions as the powerful tool nature intended them to be:

I don't say that I never feel fear before a performance, but I have learned how to channel it. This is important, to channel feelings of fear, of anxiety, to use them so they make you more sensitive.'
(*The World of the Concert Pianist*, David Duval, p. 21)

How a pounding heart can affect us

We may fear that the audience won't hear our presentation over the sound of our pounding heart, as our body directs blood to appropriate places. This increased heart rate can be loud enough to distract us.

Meryl Streep, in accepting an Oscar award for her role in the film *Kramer versus Kramer,* said: 'I can't hear what I'm saying 'cause my heart's beating so loud.' (*Meryl Streep: The Reluctant Superstar*, Diana Maychick, p. 126)

Which musician has not at some time rushed the tempo of a tricky passage? As our innate sense of tempo is measured in relation to our heartbeat, it's not surprising that we tend to rush when under pressure. This increase in heart rate and brain wave frequency combine to create confusion of tempi, making us feel overwhelmed and confused.

At such times, remember the old saying: 'Think slow in a fast movement and fast in a slow.'

How lack of visual focus can affect us

To make matters worse, our vision may blur as our pupils dilate during stressful reactions. Although this may be only momentary, according to optometrists the split-second timing needed in performance may be disturbed.

Some musicians notice frequent blurred vision during orchestral playing. Constantly looking up from the music to the conductor's beat requires a change in focal length, or 'accommodation', and this takes time to adjust. Meanwhile, we may lose our place in the music. This does not necessarily mean our vision is failing, but that stress increases any visual difficulties. Memorisation and thorough preparation add security.

Some don't like it hot

As the body works overtime we may feel flushed or sweat profusely. Pianist and cellist Juliet Hoey had this embarrassing 'red face' episode:

While performing a recorded recital, streams of perspiration caused my rather loose reading glasses to slip. The Bach fugue was a nightmare of constantly pushing them back. Twice, they actually fell off. Somehow, I struggled to the end without stopping – and had my glasses overhauled soon after.

As a clarinettist, I once tried to cover my often reddened face with slimy looking green 'correcting base' make-up. I soon abandoned this messy effort, deciding flushed faces are relatively normal for wind and brass players. Such instruments do require a reasonable amount of pressure and exertion. Shrug it off as part of the job.

The body has a built-in air conditioning system: perspiration is released to cool down the system. Ironically, as well as feeling over-warm, we may have cold and clammy hands. Icy hands hinder fluency of technique in challenging passages.

Stress can leave you breathless

I examined a clarinet-playing Diploma candidate who simply forgot to breathe. As he normally had good breath control, he was surprised at his uncharacteristic behaviour under stress. We both laughed and this released the pressure.

When threatened, spinal muscles tense the back and the diaphragm and intercostal muscles tighten. These reactions may specifically affect our normal breathing pattern, so that even trained singers and wind musicians may unconsciously hyperventilate or else hold their breath, or panic because air supply seems inadequate.

These are normal, in-built reactions geared to keep the human race intact. They are a healthy response so long as we do not remain in a state of tension for prolonged periods and are not frightened by an over-charge of adrenaline.

These responses may be activated not only when we face terrifying situations, but also when we merely think about them. When the stressful situations conglomerate into continual overload, the body systems begin to break down and we may become ill. We may feel pain in the solar plexus because the sympathetic nervous system works overtime. Back pain may result from over-stimulated glands busily pumping out adrenaline. Chapter 8 has some solutions.

Before we give up in horror, pawn our instruments and apply for jobs that don't require public performances, we should recognise that all this is normal and can be overcome.

Where the symptoms of fear come from

The physical symptoms associated with stress can be explained by the sudden rush of adrenaline released by the adrenal glands into the bloodstream. With a heightened awareness of the reactions occurring

15

during a performance, we can learn to channel these changes into a charge of energy, sharpening our perceptions and heightening our emotional and expressive powers.

Of this, pianist Jorge Bolet says:

I'm always a little bit more nervous playing in New York than anywhere else. However, I think nerves are a wonderful thing, as long as it is the kind of nerves that increases your adrenaline, sharpens your ears, gets your mind to a really fine pitch. Such nerves sharpen all the nerve endings in your fingers.

(*The World of the Concert Pianist*, David Duval, p. 85)

In some performances we find ourselves shaping phrases more exquisitely and with new depths of feeling and imagination, communicating with the audience as never before. Timing and preparedness are important. Realising that the heartbeat and brainwave activity are increased, we can learn to pace ourselves and slow down.

In fact, some excitement and even nerves are is essential to add spice and energy to a performance. Without them, it might be dull, prosaic, mere 'playing the dots'. Experienced performers learn to channel the charge of adrenaline and nervous energy to good use. Many who previously suffered agonies come to discover that they play better in performance than in the safety of their studio at home. Some healthy nerves sharpen concentration. It often happens that the section we most dreaded sparkles the brightest in the program, while there are surprising lapses in a 'safe' piece.

Often, once we start playing, the adrenaline flows and notes fall into place. Those agonising moments of anticipation were the worst. It seems that anticipation affects experienced players more than the novices, who may meet their jitters when actually on stage. Yet the former, accustomed to the flow of adrenaline, welcome it and their nerves tend to fall away with the first sounds.

Why showbusiness fears are so bad

Why are the fears which bedevil those facing performance so traumatic? Performance anxiety has a cunning trick of sneaking up on us when we least expect it, although it is usually proportional to our negative thinking beforehand. After playing to a huge auditorium

16

without a qualm last week (for we prepared ourselves well, didn't we?) we may crumple before a dozen people . . . or one influential person in the front row.

Pavarotti tells how he reacted when, as a young, inexperienced performer he saw a famous tenor, one of his idols, in the audience:

I almost passed out from nervousness. You are always frightened before singing, but to add to the usual anxiety an extra cause for worry can sometimes make the whole experience unbearable. It is these extra jolts. . . that either drive you from the field or teach you to conquer your nerves. You must learn this and, if possible, learn to harness the energy they release for your benefit. It is as much a part of learning to be a singer as learning to breathe correctly.

(*My Own Story*, Luciano Pavarotti, pp. 34-5)

Most fears are bred in our imagination, in our subconscious and in our memories of past mishaps. Why are the bad performances most clearly etched on our minds? Why do we not remember the times we played brilliantly? Why are we so hard on ourselves, so grudging of any praise? Why aren't we kinder to ourselves?

The reason is that we live in a largely critical society which expects us to succeed, while still begrudging praise. We grow up amidst a conflict between high expectations of performers on the one hand, and on the other a reluctance of parents and teachers to praise in case he or she 'gets a swollen head'. The brilliant young violinist Jascha Heifitz was not told by his mother the extent of the accolades he received for his debut; when she died thirty years later, he found the yellowing clippings amongst her papers.

That thoughtless comment or cruel nickname may stunt or twist our growth as surely as a tree deprived of light shrivels. Yet a degree of self-respect is healthy and necessary. Do our school systems sufficiently prepare and train us to be ourselves, even if this may involve standing out from the crowd? How often are the highly talented neglected or not sufficiently encouraged in our education systems? What a waste of ability!

The 'tall poppy syndrome' may cause many talented performers to hide their abilities unnecessarily for fear of being ridiculed by their peers. The genius is silhouetted out from the crowd, a loner, not marching to the same drummer, usually ahead or behind his peers. Seeing this prospect, many highly intelligent children learn to 'act dumb' for fear of suffering similar put-downs. Unlike sports people, an excess of self-confidence in the performing arts is considered suspect. Yet the pressure is applied for us to achieve high scores at school, at tertiary level, in the workforce.

In the performing arts, criticism itself is elevated to an art form, one which we must endure. Do public servants have every memo closely inspected by 'experts'? Plumbers every washer or pipe? Musicians, who live with criticism every day, often feel that every mistake, every mistuned note or rushed semiquaver is notched against them by the conductor, their teacher or the critic, who are actually paid to find fault. That second player who thinks he should be in your own principal chair can register appreciation of your slightest mistake without twitching a muscle. His ear tunes your way like a big satellite dish.

Performers are expected to accept criticism as part of the job. Yet it can be very hurtful, especially to singers or speakers. Their instrument, the voice, is part of them, not something which can be dried out and put in a case after use. It's a tough jungle where the old adage 'You're only as good as your last performance' is often all too true.

Yet even a wonderful performance is no guarantee of confidence. Success is often more threatening than failure. I remember being paralysed by lack of motivation to work after winning a competition – not because of complacency, but by the daunting expectation of having to live up to this success. Now my 'failures' would be judged by a much longer yardstick; they would be set within the context of my whole career.

Margot Fonteyn recalls that while performing in New York she was 'as ever, nervous as a cat, knowing that it is even more difficult to repeat a success than to establish it in the first place'. (*Autobiography*, p.132)

Similarly, Irving Berlin said: 'The toughest thing about success is that you've got to keep on being a success. Talent is only a starting point in this business. You've got to keep on working that talent.'

Composer Leonard Bernstein suffered creative block after the success of *West Side Story*, spurred by perfectionism to prove himself, yet fearing he could not reach such heights again. He said: 'To live with myself I have to do each thing better than I've ever done any of them before.' (*Leonard Bernstein, A Life,* Meryle Secrest, p. 238)

Everyone falls short of their own standards sometimes. Is this because many of us set unrealistically high goals? We all experience mountains, valleys and plateaux of achievement. Why do we burden ourselves by always trying to live up to our peaks?

A bio-rhythm chart shows that each person's life flows in three cycles: physical, mental and emotional. As these cycles are of different lengths, the highs and lows rhythmically ebb and flow. If we accept that today the mental and physical curves are in a low phase, we can allow ourselves an average or even a poor effort, concentrating on consolidation rather than striving for brilliance. It helps to know that next week's high will allow more scope and energy for forging ahead.

It is difficult to accept failure, especially when we may feel that our worth as a person is linked to the brilliance of each performance. Some may interpret less fervent applause or a lukewarm newspaper critique as failure, not only as a performer, but also as a person. No wonder that many performers become burdened by living up to constant high ideals!

We must accept that we cannot perform at the absolute peak of our ability all the time. A few mistakes do not signal doom, so why waste time and energy worrying ourselves into possible mishaps?

Summary

- **It's normal for any performer to occasionally experience a wide range of symptoms of fear.**
- **These symptoms of fear are all very normal reflections of our flight or fight reactions.**
- **In coping with fear it is helpful to understand how a pounding heart, lack of visual focus, perspiration and breathing impairment are caused by a rush of adrenaline. Yet this can be channelled to produce energy, focus and better performances.**

3

Brain power – how to make it work for you

The only thing we have to fear is fear itself.

Franklin D. Roosevelt

A man who fears suffering is already suffering what he fears.

Michel de Montaigne

No passion so effectually robs the mind of all its powers of acting and reasoning as fear.

Edmund Burke

ANTHROPOLOGIST MARGARET MEAD estimated that the average human utilises only four per cent of his or her potential. Others put this as low as one per cent. How much of that wastage is because our brains are clogged up with negative thoughts and worries? Many scholars have expressed the idea that our degree of achievement relates to the expectations and limitations of our thoughts.

We are what we think we are. How many times have we limited ourselves by such thoughts as: 'I just don't have good rhythm.'

Aristotle said: 'What you expect, that you shall find' and the Bible's Book of Proverbs says: 'As we think within ourselves, so we are.' How many times have we expected to botch up that tricky section, dreaded it as the moments approached, tensed up, and ... oops! Even though we resolutely vowed: 'I will get it right!' This is similar to the Biblical truth that 'Whatever a man sows, that shall he also reap' or the Eastern concept of Karma, a word that means 'Come back' in Sanskrit – that is, our thoughts and deeds come back to us.

Yet take heart. If we curb our negative thoughts, we can usually sidestep these worst scenarios. Don't we all remember days when we worked ourselves into miseries over future worries which never eventuated? Epictetus wrote in the first century AD: 'Men feel disturbed, not by things, but by the views they take of them.' Are we more daunted by the sight of these semiquavers, or by the bleak fear that our fingers cannot hold them together?

With experience and maturity, many of us do come to a reasonable self-knowledge, but we must be on guard for distortions in our thinking processes.

Don't we all know that nagging little voice that lurks in our heads, pestering us especially when great demands are placed upon us? It speaks with such conviction, predicting apocalyptic disasters out of minor hitches, that who are we to dispute it? Notice that it has all the doom and gloom of a revivalist preacher. We need ammunition against such a voice.

Thinking distortions that hamper performance

Here is the rogues' gallery of fifteen distorted thinkers who can unnecessarily make performance a nightmare:

• Filtering

The sufferer from tunnel vision. He magnifies the weaker, negative aspects of a performance, while filtering out all his positive achievements. He has an excellent memory when it comes to the glitches, hiccups, stumbles and uneven passages. Yet he stares blankly when we compliment him on his clarity of articulation, the brilliance of his fingers in the Presto or his sensitive touch. He appears unaware of his strengths.

Antidote: Bite your tongue on adjectives like 'terrible', 'awful', 'poor' and on phrases such as 'I'm no good.' Change the focus, attune your ears, put away that magnifying glass! Tape some performances and play them back later, when you can be more objective. Choose which comments, whose voices to take seriously.

• Polarised thinking

The black-and-white viewpoint. There is no middle ground, only absolutes of good and bad, success or failure. If the performance wasn't perfect, it must be a failure. Might as well give up now and save any more heartbreak.

Antidote: Think in percentages. For example: 'About thirty per cent of me is shaking, but seventy per cent is holding on and coping'; 'I played ninety-five per cent right notes'; or: 'Five per cent of the time I'm ill-prepared, but other times I'm hard working.'

• Overgeneralisation

This victim makes sweeping conclusions based on a single incident and expects future repetitions. If a fiasco happens once, she expects it to be the norm. Because she missed the top note once, she now assumes it is not in her range and labels herself a mezzo-soprano instead of a soprano.

Antidote: Banish words such as 'every', 'none', 'nobody', 'never', 'all', 'everybody'. Encourage flexible thinking with 'may', 'sometimes', 'often', 'in some cases'.

Ask: Is there any evidence for this? Does your teacher think you are a mezzo?

• Mind reading

It is risky and often incorrect to interpret audience body language or events, or to make snap judgments about people's reactions. (Surely that frowning colleague dislikes the performance!)

Antidote: Ask yourself: Have they actually said anything? Is there any evidence? Perhaps you should ask them for reassurance, especially if they are generally positive people.

• Catastrophising

This poor performer always imagines the worst. You see her holding her breath, just waiting for disaster. Her speech is littered with 'What ifs'. A thundercloud of gloom encircles her.

Antidote: Ask: Did your flu actually develop into pneumonia? Did the accompanist really forget her music? I thought you said the world was scheduled to end last Tuesday...?

• Personalisation

This victim relates everything to himself, constantly comparing himself with others. 'She can play that Scherzo faster than me; I'm just no good.' If that person in the front row looks glum, he assumes she dislikes his performance, when actually her mother died last week.

Antidote: Remember the words of the *Desiderata*: 'If you compare yourself with others, you may become vain and bitter for always there will be greater and lesser persons than yourself.' You are unique … be yourself.

• **Control fallacies**

There are two aspects here: the person who views himself as being helpless, a victim of fate. Or, at the other extreme, one who thinks herself omnipotent and responsible for those around her, carrying the weight of the world on her shoulders.

Antidote: Think: I make it happen; I am responsible for myself, my colleagues for themselves. This is my life.

• **Fallacy of fairness**

Trying to apply legal or contractual rules to the vagaries of personal relationships often means making conditional assumptions: 'If she really believed me to be a good singer, she would have asked me to sing at her wedding.' Or: 'If I really had talent, I'd be playing principal, not second'.

As other people rarely view the situation in the same way, this person is constantly hurt by their reactions. In fact, her favourite word, 'fair', is a misnomer for what she wants from them and from life.

Antidote: Be honest with yourself and with others by saying this is what you 'want', not what is 'fair'.

• **Fallacy of change**

This person expects other people to change if he pressures them enough by blaming, withholding, demanding, trading or arguing. He knows all the tricks in the book and turns his disappointments on others, thinking that his happiness depends on their actions (whereas it depends on the thousands of small and large decisions he makes through his life).

Antidote: Tell him: Your happiness depends on you and the many large and small decisions you make. You are responsible for yourself; I am responsible for me.

• Emotional reasoning

Feelings are not realistic indicators of performance. If she feels clumsy or slow or incompetent, then of course she is clumsy or slow or incompetent. Regardless of what we tell her, she won't listen. She relies so heavily on her emotions that she lives a depressed life.

Antidote: Feelings can lie, so examine them before allowing them to control you.

• Global labelling

It is equally risky to generalise one or two qualities into a sweeping negative global judgment, taking a grain of truth to mean the whole picture. Such a person labels that introverted musician 'dumb', the director 'a bully and megalomaniac'. These judgments are usually false because they focus on a single characteristic or example or behaviour, but they imply that it's the whole picture.

Antidote: Ask yourself: Is my description always true, true only now, or true only some of the time? Be specific.

• Blaming

Some people are adept at making other people responsible for their inadequacies, faults and decisions. Thus – it was his teacher's fault that he was not ready for the audition. A less confident person, on the other hand, blames herself for everything, constantly knocking herself as incompetent and always ill-prepared, no matter how she slaves at practising. She would never enter a competition because she could not imagine winning.

Antidote: Both types of blaming can be covered by these statements: 'I am responsible for my own decisions. I accept that I made a mistake. I don't have to be perfect.'

• 'Shoulds'

This person feels guilty if she doesn't measure up to her high standards and angry with those who break the rules. 'I should never have made a silly mistake like that! If only I'd got out of bed an hour earlier to warm-up more ...' Her thoughts and speech are peppered with words like 'should' and 'ought', revealing too rigid, inflexible rules.

Antidote: Be flexible in rules and values, for there are always exceptional and special circumstances. Think of three exceptions to your rule. Ban the words 'should', 'ought' and 'must'.

- **'Being right'**

Selective deafness results from his need to be always right and relationships suffer because colleagues resent these attitudes. He is compelled to prove continually that his ideas and actions are correct. He is defensive and hates to be proved wrong. ('Who, me? Wrong notes in the fugue? Rubbish! You're tone-deaf; how would you know?')

Antidote: Listen to others! Most situations contain many possibilities and many answers.

- **'Heaven's reward' fallacy**

This victim has slaved at her career, her responsibilities, on the understanding that all the hard work, sacrifice and self-denial must pay off in the 'ever after'. She practises endlessly, diligently doing the 'right' things, like several hours' scale practice before breakfast. She is such a burned-out wreck physically and emotionally that she cannot project musically in concerts and does not reap the benefits of her work.

Antidote: Get a life! Program some enjoyable time each day to replenish yourself through relationships and recreation. Live in the present.

How our mind can work for us

When we become aware of distorted automatic thoughts, we don't have to let them overgrow our minds like noxious fungus. We can acknowledge them, which is far preferable to sweeping them into a dark corner and hoping that they will shrivel and die. Then block them with proactive positive thoughts:

- **'I don't have to think this. I've allowed my thoughts to get into this rut.' Or try a Shakespearean touch: 'Out, vile thought!'**
- **Blot out the thoughts by thinking positively, or just**

repeating one word over and over such as 'sing sing sing'.

- Think: 'Stop!' to block the thoughts – or shout it aloud if necessary.
- Imagine yourself at the console of a recording studio. Turn down the volume of those negative voices; even edit them right out. Lift the volume of your grandmother, who thinks you are so clever. Or your teacher's voice saying 'You've worked hard this week. Well done!'

Many top sports stars vouch that the strength of a performance relies on their mental preparation. In the performing arts we need to use this important tool more often. If you feed your mind with pictures of success, failure is less likely.

Is it foolproof? There are many factors involved – technique, adequate rehearsal, readiness for the challenge. The great cellist Gregor Piatagorsky, asked how he helped pre-performance nerves, said he constantly reminded himself: 'You are the great Piatagorsky.' – 'And does it help?' – 'No, I don't believe myself!' (*Notes From the Green Room*, Salmon Paul, p. 34.)

The Queensland Orchestra trumpeter Paul Rawson explains how he helps his students:

I don't teach students to 'psych' themselves or to relax, but instead to enjoy the tension, to use the adrenaline and to redirect it into focus on the occasion. I tell myself that any tension is a percentage taken from my concentration. If I feel tension I think, Ah, I'm not concentrating and I redirect the energy.

Once I was called in at short notice to deputise for a concert which was to be broadcast live. As I drove in through traffic jams, I just focused on my concentration, trying to build it up to the full hundred per cent. I performed with no nerves whatsoever, no tension, just one wrong note which didn't faze me at all.

Program your mind securely in the preparation stages (more on this in Chapter 5) and you will be surprised at the strength of its response under pressure. Check your reactions against those described in Chapter 4 and then apply the suggested coping mechanisms.

How the brain works

Understanding how the brain works can help us to counter fear.

The brain can act in different modes. When we feel threatened in a high-risk situation like performance, the more primitive section of the brain takes over. This resembles that of reptiles, to whom survival, a speedy escape from danger, strength and the quick strike are basic. This 'reptilian' brain regulates our breathing and our heartbeat and maintains equilibrium and muscle tone. We have already noted that these very aspects are most likely to be affected in stressful situations. When our body is revved up to meet the challenges, our heart beats faster, breathing is restricted and the mouth dries.

At the same time, a more sophisticated part of the brain, the cerebral cortex, with which we reason, think and speak, seems to be shutting down. 'I just couldn't think straight,' we say. Our reptilian brain is taking charge, overwhelming the cerebral cortex.

We need to learn to slow down internally, to systematically condition ourselves to deal with the instinctive responses of the reptilian brain. By deliberately slowing those survival responses, we can make them work for us instead of against us. We can access the frontal lobes and coherent thought by slow deep breathing and Brain Gym actions such as those outlined in Chapter 8. This enables us to control our instincts to a degree that makes it possible for us to manage this level of excitement so that we are still able to think clearly on our feet.

Many are alarmed by the tension that floods our bodies, but it can be channelled to positive use. Compare it to electricity. If we harness it, we have great resources of power available. The absence of all tension may result in boring, matter-of-fact performance, lacking the vitality to engross the listener. The audience may be alienated, perceiving a sense of complacence or arrogance on the part of the performer.

If we fight the waves when surfing, we struggle, swallow salt-water and may be roughly dumped. But wait for the next wave, watch it build up. Catch it on the crest, go with it, allow its power to sweep us along. Frightening? No. Exhilarating!

Summary

- The fight or flight response can be channelled from unnerving symptoms into energy. Thus the negative physical effects are lessened.
- The mind has enormous power to influence our actions and can be harnessed to our good. There are specific ways in which our minds can play tricks on us by giving negative messages, and ways we can 'psych' ourselves by receiving positive messages.

4

Positive strategies for coping with fear

Then fancies fly away,
I'll fear not what men say,
I'll labour night and day
To be a pilgrim.

John Bunyan, 17th-century
nonconformist preacher

PEOPLE REACT TO FEAR SITUATIONS in many different ways. These are not usually very helpful, but be assured: none of them is deadly.

Undeadly sins of reaction

Many of us have experienced some or all of these seven unhelpful reactions:

• Fight or flight

The caveman challenged by a bear could grab his spear or run away. But we performers know we'll be lucky to receive a second chance if we rabbit off the stage in mid-concert.

• Les miserables

A common reaction is to torture ourselves in the days before by obsessively mulling on the worst possible consequences: 'I'll forget the words, dry up and the audience will boo me off stage.' Or we may gear our thinking to distort and rationalise the fear: 'I'll forget, of course, because I had a memory lapse that first time I sang it five years ago.' Some of us cannot cope because of focusing on our feelings of fright.

Many martyrs suffer their nerves in miserable silence, perhaps displaying commendable modesty and self-effacement in allowing lesser players the opportunities so they themselves can avoid challenges: 'No, Jane should take the lead role; she projects better.' The time is never quite right for tackling that tricky concerto or tough role: better save it for my maturity … and so on until the retirement villa looms.

• Robots anonymous

One escape hatch is to block out all thoughts and perform in a *non compos*, zombie state, mercifully unconscious of what happens in the performance. Joanne Wolfe, one of my students, describes on pages 35 and 36 how she used this coping technique for years. We were both pleased when she told me she was able to play a performance fully aware, remembering both the glitches as well as the beautiful passages. She played as a person, not a robot, projecting her own feelings, imagination and ideas, rather than mechanical strings of notes.

• The artful dodger

We can become adept at dodging with conviction. One safe method is to fall prey to a noxious virus which necessitates postponing or putting in a deputy.

• Procrastination

Many performers display powers in procrastination: 'I'll start serious work after the long weekend, no point before!' We almost avoid the agony, but by putting off the necessary preparation, we only make the end result more insecure and probably the performance fares worse than our abilities might warrant.

• Avoidance

Sufferers of acute stage fright may finally avoid playing altogether. While this may reduce the discomfort initially, our self-esteem suffers: instead of controlling our fears, the fears control us.

• The buck stops … elsewhere!

'If only I had more preparation time … my teacher hadn't made me play that particular piece, I wasn't ready for it … if only I wasn't sick last week. If I hadn't been distracted by that heckler/rustling program in the front row … if John hadn't played the same piece faster/louder …'

In other words, if I can find something or someone else to blame, I won't have to lift my game. But then, I shan't improve until I face up to the responsibility that I have the same number of hours in a day as everyone else, that it is my life and my performance, my fingers or my breath that play or speak. Until I accept that I am what I am, warts, talents and all, then I'll never really master my problems. Only then can I make some headway with improving myself and my situations.

• **Become detached from the audience**

We can try to pretend that the audience is not there, like the monkey who sees no evil. This may be a reasonable coping mechanism, but at the expense of failing to communicate empathy and rich imagination to an impressed audience. At best it may result in a bland, acceptable effort. Besides, a cough or squirm will soon remind us of the existence of that audience. Instead, try facing them in the ways suggested below.

We all need some protective coping mechanisms sometimes for bare survival. However, these largely negative reactions do not allow us to develop our full potential, nor our careers to forge ahead. Surely there are positive reactions that we can utilise?

As much as we might like it to be otherwise, we all fail at times – even the best of us. American actor Harrison Ford has said: 'Failures are inevitable. Unfortunately, in film, they live forever and they're forty feet wide and twenty feet high.' At least musical performances are less permanent! IBM founder Thomas Watson said: 'In order to succeed, double your failure rate.'

Some hints for reacting positively to fear

There are, fortunately, some positive strategies for coping with fear. They include:

• **Confront fears**

A most important initial step is to acknowledge the stress or tension. It will then loosen its stranglehold. Face, confront and admit those fears. Free flow of expression is blocked if we do not do so. Many hope to jolly themselves out of their morass, to wish away their

31

ostrich, they bury their heads in the sand until problems

Hardly a comfortable performance posture.

sponse from performers who were asked 'How do you prevent stage fright?'– 'Prepare! Practise thoroughly and with plenty of time!' More in-depth consideration will be given to this in Chapter 5. See also the author's *Practice is a Dirty Word; How to clean up your act.*

• Experience breeds confidence

Forcing oneself into frequent performance opportunities develops confidence. 'Hey, I survived! I got to the end! I did it!' It's far harder to stoke oneself up for occasional performances than to face numerous routine ones.

Singer Rhonda Bruce writes:

After a career of isolated solo performances, a role in a long-running musical was a relief. As I became so used to going on stage every single night, it ceased to be a major event and became as easy as any familiar, routine job.

Russian violinist David Oistrakh said: 'If one plays less than twice a month, it could crack anyone's nerves.' *(Great Violinists in Performance,* Henry Roth, p. 74)

• Reverse roles

Anxious performers feel exposed, vulnerable, on display. Try reversing the situation – imagine the audience or jury panel huddling in their underwear, even naked. You'll feel self-assured by comparison.

Eloise Riisted, working with nervous musicians, used such humour to defuse the power of critics. She asked them to imagine in caricature the debilitating 'judges' of their minds and strip off their robes. Then watch them scurry, naked, for cover. As they laughed them away, those judges lost much of their power.

• Shift the focus of attention

You can resolutely haul your attention elsewhere. Sit comfortably relaxed and visualise transferring all your nervous energy away from the tense part of your body (for example, the jaw) down into your toes.

In performance, think 'toes, toes, toes', and the jaw relaxes. Practise this in the weeks before a performance. When you feel worried about tricky fingering, transfer your attention to deep breathing and the fingers will flow with ease.

• **Physically relax and use breathing exercises**

Chapter 7 deals with some of the many possibilities: relaxation and meditation techniques, yoga, Feldenkreis and Dalcroze methods, breathing exercises and more.

• **Focus on a benevolent stranger in the audience**

This is preferable to detachment and will draw a positive response from the audience. Choose a pleasant face from the crowd and make that person's day by playing just for him or her.

• **Identify with the audience**

Tell yourself: 'If all these cultured/discerning/important people have come here tonight to hear me perform, then I must really be worth hearing.' As success breeds success, so a positive attitude earns respect from a majority.

• **The paradoxical approach**

Some performers consciously make their hands tremble, their knees shake or their palms sweat as a way of trying to produce the symptom rather than conceal it. Clarinettist and guitarist Karlin Love says:

> *Because I have so much mental energy going on in a performance, it helps me to focus on one finger as it's virtually impossible to think about all of them at once. In my case, I concentrate on curving the left hand fourth finger. The result is that my fingers stop shaking or, at least, the shaking doesn't interfere with my playing. I also find it helpful to practise slowly and correctly, feeling the passage through to form an accurate memory. In later performances, I remember how that felt …*

This is surprisingly difficult! Other performers may deliberately commit a small mistake, thereby fulfilling that fear of a clanger, thus heading off further anxiety. Now the mistake is over and done with, they cease to fear a total fiasco.

• Self-program

Program yourself for a successful performance by visualising it in detail weeks before the event. Create a self-fulfilling prophecy.

• Become absorbed in the performance

The more we love our work, and the more we invest in sharing the treasures of our art, the less we are aware of stage fright. The great acting teacher Stanislavski said: 'Love the art in yourself, not yourself in the art.' Focusing on ourselves exacerbates our problems: we need to look outwards. Violist/composer Brett Dean says:

> *Performing in a large ensemble or a concerto is easier; there are a lot of people behind you to help. I find it helps me to look at the score before playing, to realise I'm just one of many other musicians. And eye contact with my colleagues helps. I try to create contact, so I open out rather than close in on myself.*

• Use your imagination

Shift your mind away from the worries. Infuse colour and vitality into your performance by inventing a storyline to fit the moods you project. Assign voices and characters to the parts, invent dialogues in your mind between, for example, a big-booted macho tenor and an eyelash-batting soprano. Or imagine the colours and textures of various instruments: a rich, deep bronze cello in this phrase, a bright silver piccolo there.

Such ideas improve focus, concentration, projection and enjoyment.

• Give out

Giving out to others switches the spotlight off our own fears. Help someone else and your own nerves will seem less constricting. Help the audience to appreciate your performance.

• Enjoy!

Much of my own teaching consists of encouraging students to enjoy their music. Our society and institutions, our performing arts centres are riddled with industrious, conscientious little ants, busily developing technique, practising fanatically and endlessly, taking themselves and their music so seriously. They are pushed on by their teachers' high expectations and criticisms.

It is tragic that many lose the enjoyment of their art. Worse, in this great fog, they may miss the moods, the emotions – even the humour – that the composer or playwright wanted expressed.

British violinist Nigel Kennedy was scathing of one institution:

> *There is the stench of ambition, of ruthless professional people only too happy to conform to whatever is musically suitable to succeed. It must be heartbreaking for composers … Mr Great Composer sweated blood to get his feelings out and, centuries later, audiences make a conscious effort to try and recapture the fullness of that man's passion.*
>
> (Always Playing, Nigel Kennedy, p. 18.)

Many classical composers had a wonderful sense of humour. I cannot play music by Franz Krommer with a straight face, for he frequently intersperses comic leaps like hiccups. Malcolm Arnold, who scored his Grand, Grand Overture for soloists playing vacuum cleaners and floor polishers, certainly did not want us to take music so seriously.

Look for the beauty, the composer's craftsmanship, the wit and sparkle and the difficulties will be easier to face. Then panic, tension, fear of criticism or of tripping will fade to manageable proportions. If you enjoy the music so will the listeners.

Clarinettist Joanne Wolfe encapsulates many of these points in telling how she conquered her own 'White faces' experiences:

> *I was plagued by stage fright as a teenager and through half of my tertiary study. I would avoid performing where possible. When I did perform, my mind would shut down to protect me from the barrage of emotions and anxieties, leaving me playing on automatic. At times, I would walk on stage and the next I knew the audience would be applauding. I have no recollection at all of many performances. A lack of perspective was my biggest problem: I thought every performance was going to make or break me.*
>
> *After confronting these unacknowledged fears and reducing them to normal perspective, for the first time I could clearly remember a performance in my second year at university, how it felt and sounded, how the audience reacted. For once, I truly communicated the music instead of just playing the dots. Now, I quite enjoy playing.*

My advice is to be prepared, both emotionally and technically, and to maintain perspective. No single performance, exam or audition is the be-all and end-all of your career. One botched concert will not destroy you.

Lastly, revel in the music you make, but not as a vehicle for your ego. You are a channel for the music. The music, not you, is paramount.

Summary

- **Many of our strategies for coping with stress in fact block free communication.**

- **Strategies which can help include confronting our fears, preparing well, relaxation and breathing techniques, self-programming and more. Absorption in and enjoyment of the music allow performers to forget nerves and communicate to their audience.**

Part B

Solutions

How to prepare for a confident performance

Fail to prepare = prepare to fail.

Anonymous

The readiness is all.

William Shakespeare,
Hamlet, Act V

Unless you work as hard as the peasants in the field, you cannot call yourself an artist.

Vincent van Gogh

SO MANY PEOPLE CAN'T BE WRONG! When I asked a wide cross-section of musicians: 'What helps you cope with performance tensions?' their first response was almost invariably: 'Preparation!'

There is no substitute for thorough preparation

We do reap what we sow. If we know, submerged deep down under the procrastinations, avoidances, excuses and distracting trivia, that we have neglected solid preparation, some nerves are as inevitable as Monday follows Sunday. Performance fears are surely lessened when we have prepared securely and wisely in the months before the performance.

We can program our brains like a computer, feeding in correct information concerning hand positions, the sequence of notes, or fingering. Then, if a blur of panic overwhelms us in the initial moments of a performance, we can safely go into 'auto-drive' for a few moments. We know that our brain is securely programmed and will send messages to our lips or fingers without our consciously driving them.

Herein lies confidence. Yet if in the initial preparation stages we learned mistakes or clumsy fingerings into a passage, then such weaknesses will surface when we deliver under stress.

The first aural and visual impressions will be your strongest, those your memory will retain. Ensure that they are accurate and clear impressions. Next day, your brain has only to remember, not relearn. From now on, practice is a relatively simple process of consolidation.

Often as a student I learned new music too hastily, cementing in foreign notes and stumbles. I'm amazed how strongly those first impressions were etched into my subconscious. Even after hours of diligent, intelligently applied rehearsal techniques, an early mistake still clings like suction in my mind. Playing the same piece twenty years later, even with a new, pristine copy of the music, my mind and fingers often hesitate, falter, stumble, drawn irresistibly to that fault learned in a moment's careless reading. What a waste of some beautiful repertoire, pock-marked with mindless mistakes!

Thus we see that a secure preparation process is of high priority in ensuring successful presentations. Let us work together for your next performance or presentation through this very important learning process.

Put that last fiasco behind you. Its sound has long died. It is over and can never be recaptured in time. Throw away the memory tangibly! Write down on a piece of paper your own particular bogey – 'September audition' or 'recording', perhaps a few details that still rankle at the back of the mind. Now, screw up the paper, throw it in the bin or burn it. We are going to work together on your next exciting performance project. Let's tackle this right from the essential foundations.

The practice routine for the weeks ahead

In aiming for the perfect performance, we often focus on that big goal, the concert, and forget the importance of the spadework where the seeds are sown. There are two essentials for confident performance:

• **A secure technical foundation, built up through daily**

conscientious, thinking practice, guided by a capable teacher.

• **Careful preparation of your score or part.**

An old saying goes: 'The amateur practises until he can get it right, the professional until he can't get it wrong.' You have a new piece or concerto to learn. Let's take this necessary process right from the beginning.

Practise the work at a slow pace

'One must practise slowly, then more slowly, and finally slowly' said Camille Saint-Saëns, reputed as an organist and pianist as well as a composer.

Samuel Johnson wrote that what we hope to do with ease, we must first do with diligence. During the early learning stages of tackling a new work, the bulk of practice should be at a slow tempo, as comfortable and rhythmic as a rocking chair. Zipping through the score dragging fingers and brain behind causes tensions, missed connections, confusions.

Play new music at half-speed. To see progress, practise with a metronome, each day moving it one or two notches faster, so that the fingers and brain don't even notice any increase in speed. After a few weeks, with the speed even faster than that needed in performance, there is room for relaxation. Now you can play fast and fluently, with a minimum of tension.

Practise the work silently

Another valuable learning technique involves voicing the notes before you actually play them. Say the notes aloud as you finger through the piece, before actually playing a note out aloud. Tap or clap the rhythm.

Work in bite-sized bits

When challenged with short segments, the brain can keep up with any demands. So often we practise in huge chunks, reading through whole pages rather than breaking it down to bite-sized bits.

Working in small units, the brain can concentrate – relax –

concentrate – relax. Just as the rhythm of the waves ebbs back and forth while progressively drawing further out to sea, so our technique can be stretched, then relaxed, in order to challenge further until soon the whole page is mastered.

Sandy Walker, Brisbane pianist and teacher, says:

Another fun way of practising is from the outside in! Start with learning the first bar and the last bar. Then, bar 2 and the second last bar. Cement 1 and 2 together and then second last and last. Then, learn bar 3 and cement it to 1 and 2; likewise, the last three bars. Soon, you will find yourself in the middle of the piece and, hey presto! You have learnt the rest.

Set the goal posts

We all need to set clear goals to keep ourselves motivated. By setting and reaching for goals, we take charge of our lives, rather than allowing life to take charge of us. But sometimes we aim too high, miss and give up.

Break large goals into smaller, bite-sized parts. Map out lists of short-term, medium-term and long-term goals. Relish the satisfaction of crossing off goals as they are achieved. Ask yourself each day what is the most important aspect needing your time, energy and work. A steady, regular practice routine is far more effective than fits and starts.

Note your progress

Keeping a journal or practice notebook is very valuable, both for planning time usage in advance and also to look back later and see how much you have improved. Read through a scrapbook of your press clippings and reports to boost self-esteem on the days when improvement seems minuscule.

Sit down with your notebook well before the big event to map out a program, listing the technical/musical problems this involves. Write a list of goals. Within each time slot, allow yourself several minutes of relaxation, movement, a breath of fresh air, a drink of water. You will then use work time more efficiently and minimise risk of repetitive strain injury. Again, give yourself the satisfaction of crossing goals off the list when they are reached. Reward yourself with a pat on the back or a treat.

Memorise the task

Singers and pianists take memorisation for granted. Most other musicians manage to avoid memorisation unless their sights are set on the concert and competition circuit. Certainly it should be encouraged, as one is better able to focus on the music when it is thoroughly internalised. If the eyes blur in performance due to pupil dilation, it is reassuring to fall back on memory.

Melbourne singer Rhonda Bruce says about this:

When graduating from Juilliard School of Music, I performed a Mozart aria to many distinguished personages. I became so nervous that my conscious mind completely lost the words. To my own astonishment, I heard myself singing the words anyway, seemingly without having thought them first! From this I realised what it means to have memorised a part totally. If it's possible to forget, then one hasn't indelibly memorised it!

The practice routine during the days before

If you have begun your preparation early enough, practice time should consist of consolidation rather than panic-pushing. Play or speak through the whole without stopping several times each day. If you can manage that speech or concerto three times through in quick succession, your stamina will surely cope with one performance on the night!

A large proportion of average practice time consists of stop-start work. We need to balance this with a view of the big picture, discovering the concentration and stamina needed to perform it as a whole.

Perform dummy runs

Enlist supportive colleagues – Grandma, Aunty Marge and the budgie – to listen to a dummy-run of the performance at a specified time. Treat it as a real performance, gearing yourself through the day, quietening yourself and focusing beforehand. Barbara Jane Gilby, violin lecturer at the Canberra School of Music, suggests:

I play my piece through at home, often wearing the performance clothes, with the radio or television turned up quite loud, to check my memorisation and to develop the ability to concentrate in adverse conditions.

Play to pleasant, non-judgmental people at a retirement village or kindergarten. Your local church might welcome meditative music during communion, or a rousing finale to send people on their way. Such audiences will really appreciate your giving time and talents for their enjoyment.

Play often and each time any agonies will lessen. You will surprise yourself by coping better and improving each time.

We tread a fine line in timing the readiness of a work for an important performance. Ideally, we should learn it slowly and comfortably, improving it for a performance in a relatively non-threatening situation. Here, we take careful note of any mishaps, for they signal the weak spots which will need concentrated work before other test flights. Then put the piece aside for a few weeks to prevent staleness – even better, for some months. At our next foray, we can approach it with fresh perspective and enthusiasm, building up to a peak for the big performance.

Rehearse in the venue of the performance

Try to book the particular auditorium for a prior rehearsal, or at least a short practice-run. This is invaluable to grow accustomed to the acoustics and feel of the hall, while allowing that an empty hall is more resonant than one filled with people.

Ask a colleague to listen to this rehearsal to give an objective appraisal of balance and ascertain whether the sound projects to the back of the hall. Reed players should test several prepared reeds in the auditorium, choosing the one which responds best in the particular acoustic.

Get the most out of the rehearsal

Rehearse more than adequately with the pianist or other players. Where possible, schedule rehearsals to begin well before the performances to ensure plenty of time for adjustment and consolidation.

Singers and solo recitalists soon learn to value a supportive, reliable accompanist. Treasure the one who breathes and thinks with you, who will jump bars to follow any memory lapses or confusions. It is important to allow plenty of rehearsal time rather than rely on his or her powers of extrasensory perception. Be specific in asking for help with cues for entries or pitching notes.

Sydney singer Leonie McMahon can vouch for this:

There I was, singing away through a difficult opening. My next section had already started when I realised the organist (who was an inexperienced accompanist) had left me without an entry cue. I tried to get in, but couldn't pitch the note without the normal help I had come to expect from my usual accompanists. I waited for him to repeat the entry and collect me second time round. But no, he was doing his own thing and hadn't even noticed I wasn't with him.

The first note missed, the second, the third, seconds ticking away like a time bomb. It couldn't be happening to me; there had been no trouble in rehearsal! The tenor tried to hum the note for me. Finally, I came in on the major keynote where I felt safe.

The tremendous spurt of adrenaline coursing through my veins kept me going without collapsing. My knees wobbled, but they held me up. My voice didn't waver, though my breath was fast and panting. I remember going into the calmness of shock while my mind repeated, 'This too shall pass away'.

My greatest achievement was that I kept going when I wanted to burst into tears. In later performances, I felt comforted that I had overcome my nerves enough to proceed. It also taught me how spoilt I was with my previous excellent accompanists.

Give clear up-beats or nods to bring in the pianist at the tempo you really mean, practising opening entries several times. Know exactly what tempo you want. Before beginning, take a few moments to silently sing through the first phrase to establish the tempo at which you are comfortable. Rehearsal is essential, even or especially if the pianist has played the work many times before, to establish that it really is your tempo and not that of the previous performers.

What if the pianist sets the wrong tempo in an introduction?

Frantic gestures and beating the air destroy the mood, your own poise and the audience's enjoyment. Simply allow the pianist to continue playing the intro, then begin resolutely at the speed you really want and expect the accompanist to follow you. Be careful that you do not give mixed signals such as a toe tapping at a completely different tempo.

What if I come unstuck from my pianist mid-piece?

If you make a mistake, keep going rhythmically and rely on the pianist to find you. If you wander back to pick up that lost note or beat, you may both grope for each other in the frightening fog of no-man's land. Most pianists soon learn to jump a beat, bar or line without the slightest flicker to give the game away. After all, the solo line is written in their score. They accept that it is their role to reconnoitre, yours to lead.

Such possibilities are lessened if you know the music thoroughly – both your part and, equally importantly, the piano part. Listen to recordings and live performances of the work. Practise from the score so you can see what is going on. I find it reassuring to pencil in crucial rhythmic cues so that I know what to listen for.

You can keep your pianist on-side and save rehearsal time-wastage with some simple preparations. Experienced Brisbane accompanist Sue Witham suggests:

- **Give or send the music to your accompanist at least two weeks before the performance.**
- **Mark your breathing points in the piano score.**
- **Mark any tempo and dynamic changes or extra ones.**
- **Acknowledge your accompanist at the end of the performance. The piano part is often as demanding as the solo part, if not more so!**
- **On a practical level, note the time, date and place of the performance on paper, perhaps on the music.**
- **Ask what the fee will be and have it ready after the performance. Treat your accompanists in a**

professional manner and they will be happy to work with you again.

Value a good accompanist. Never take them for granted or 'ride them'. Famous accompanist Gerald Moore wrote:

> *A certain singer had me reduced to such a state of nervousness that I could hardly play the introduction to the simplest song at the start of a program without wrong notes: my fingers quivered as if with ague, my heels rat-tatted on the floor. Such was the state of mind that playing the piano was a torture to me.*
>
> *Bowing to his audience after his first song, under the noise of the applause he would turn and snarl at me with smiling moveless lips, but with a baleful glitter in his eyes which only I could see: 'Come along, come along, wake up, man. What's the matter with you?' White of face, I sat there wondering what was the matter with me.*

(Am I too Loud? Gerald Moore, p. 35-6)

Plan your timing

Plan the timing of the last days, rescheduling where possible other tiring commitments to lighten the big day. Don't feel guilty about being as lazy as possible on the day of a big challenge as long as a sensible practice routine is maintained.

The pace of our society has sped up considerably. The earlier master soloists like Heifitz, Toscanini and Rubenstein relaxed during the sea voyages en route to their concert tours. In our frenetic society, artists swot the next score or part on the flight, dragging their jet lag like a ball and chain through the first rehearsals.

Practise stage presentation

Especially if you are less experienced at performing, it is essential to practise stage presentation, guided by a teacher or experienced colleague. While you familiarise yourself with the routine you increase your own poise and preparedness. The audience will respond to the positive impression you project. Prepare all clothing in advance: a scorch mark on your shirt an hour before a performance sabotages calm.

Maintain good health

Regular swimming or other exercise helps tense muscles. Rest as much as possible. Even short catnaps help in coping with a busy schedule. Eat regular meals of nutritious food and restrict caffeine, nicotine and alcohol intake.

Have a time of quiet the night before

Not much use to suggest an early night in bed when there is probably a rehearsal. Resist the temptation, however, to go out for a drink afterwards. It is better to curl up with an undemanding book and a warm milk or herbal drink after a hot tub, in order to wind-down at bedtime. If worry sabotages your sleep, see Chapter 7.

Suggestions for the morning of the performance

It's important to be at your best when it really counts, at whatever hour. If you record at 10am, you will have to wake early enough to warm-up, prepare and arrive poised, in time to check the acoustics before the recording begins.

What a pity that all performers cannot soft-pedal themselves much as singers manage to, especially soloists! Many performers have to attend a morning rehearsal and then catch up on teaching.

However, if at all possible, follow Pavarotti's advice:

On the day of a performance, I sleep as late as I can and go to pains to avoid being awakened before my body has taken all the sleep it possibly can use ... After I am fully awake and refreshed, I vocalise seriously for two minutes. If the voice is there, I stop and relax until it is time to eat. If it is not there, I still stop after two minutes relax, then eat. I pass the time painting, perhaps reading. I avoid seeing people; talking is hard on my voice.

(*My Own Story*, Luciano Pavarotti, p. 199-200)

Most agree that exhaustive rehearsal work is counter-productive on the day of the performance. Start with some favourite exercises, then easy, comfortable practice.

The pianist Ferruccio Busoni would usually play his whole program from beginning to end, slowly, without expression. He learned that it is important to save emotional energy on the day when he once played with great excitement in rehearsal and then produced a lifeless performance that night.

How do other professionals handle the pre-concert hours? Pianist Jean-Marie Darre prefers this routine:

> *The day of the concert I think more than I play. And I like before*
> *the concert to sleep about two hours. I can sleep when I want.*
> *Sleeping is good for the nerves. If I don't have to travel all day, I*
> *practise in the morning for one or one-and-a-half hours on*
> *technique and I play all the program slowly. But sometimes I*
> *arrive [with] only time to try the piano. If I have only a half hour,*
> *I play technique on the piano and try some piece of the program.*
>
> (*Pianists at Play*, Dean Elder, p. 68)

Pianists feel more secure if they have allowed time to try out the touch of a strange piano. It may save them from even greater embarrassment. John Ogden once strode on-stage, acknowledged the applause ... then slunk off to wait for the piano to be unlocked.

We can all learn from actors and singers who know to 'save themselves' as well as their voices on the day of a performance. They talk less, eat less, pamper themselves a little and don't rush around. They retreat into themselves, focus on their part or persona and especially avoid arguments or upsets.

Coping with the hours before the performance

Take it easy, while still keeping occupied enough that your mind does not tease you with 'if onlys' and 'what ifs'. Organise any equipment that you will need well in advance – clothes, spare reeds, strings, music stands. Check your instrument is in reliable working order. There is nothing more unnerving than to discover as you walk on stage that your instrument has developed a mechanical problem. It is especially frustrating if ten minutes with a screwdriver would have fixed it. Saxophonist and clarinettist Paul Harvey writes:

> *I suffer from anxiety about instrument mechanics going wrong –*
> *springs breaking, pads falling out and so on. I have nightmares in*
> *which I open my case and there's no mouthpiece. It's not the*
> *audience I'm afraid of; it's the instrument!*
>
> *On the way to concerts, I stop the car and look in the boot to*
> *check in all the instrument cases. This worry has worsened as I*

get older. Now, I make sure everything is ready well in time, with a
spare instrument, several mouthpieces and hundreds of reeds,
pads, elastic bands and tools to hand.

A few hours before performing, eat a light meal of carbohydrate, which represents slow-release energy. This should contain a minimum of fat or oil. If you cannot face eating, suck glucose lozenges and drink Glucodin to keep up your energy levels or eat chocolate (not recommended for singers and public speakers, however, as it causes phlegm).

My violinist husband eats little before performing. As a clarinettist, I find it necessary to eat something fairly solid so that I am not inhibited by thunderous stomach rumbles each time I breathe.

Guitarist Julian Bream writes:

If I don't eat something before the concert, I'll be a nervous wreck
about halfway through. I really will. I'm so jittery I really do need
some ballast in order to do the concert at all ... if I'm getting
hungry, I get nervous and begin to make silly mistakes. Well, that's
no way to play a concert. So there's often a constant supply of
sandwiches backstage.

(A Life on the Road, Julian Bream, p. 18)

Whereas, conductor Herbert Blomstedt says:

I eat the biggest meal in the morning at 7 am, a very good meal at
noon, and at 6 pm just a little. I eat this way every day, which
means that after a concert I'm not hungry and it gives me the
opportunity to go straight to bed and I sleep immediately.
However, if you're hungry and eat after the concert, your evenings
get very drawn out and that's not healthy with this type of
schedule.

(Conductors in Conversation, Jeannine Wagar, p. 8)

Rest if possible. If you can't sleep, try reading a light book for a while in the fresh air and sunshine. Go for a walk, meditate or pray. Tension is energy which is blocked. Release it in whichever way works best for you. Go for a run or other exercise. Many people find they perform well if they are just slightly tired physically.

A long soak in the bath is wonderfully relaxing, even more so with various herbal oils or mineral salts. Water is a well-known therapy proved from Roman times. Even a five-minute bath or a quick hot shower unravels muscle tension.

Aim to arrive at a new venue with enough time to find it and to allow for any last-minute hitches. Above all, avoid rushing. On the other hand, hanging around for hours backstage can be unsettling, although some people thrive on the atmosphere.

Paul Harvey writes again:

My other recurring nightmare is where I'm late for a show in a strange theatre. I can hear the orchestra, but don't know the way to the pit. This happened to me once – while awake! – at La Scala, Milan. (Luckily, it was only a rehearsal.) I blundered through labyrinthine subterranean corridors, thinking, 'This is my nightmare; when I find the pit, there will be no mouthpiece in the case'.

Barbara Jane Gilby is realistic about nerves being part of her life:

I'd rather feel nervous some hours before a performance than sail along perfectly okay, only to have it hit me a few seconds before I play. If I'm nervous a few seconds beforehand, at least I know what I'm dealing with, and there's always the possibility the jitters will disappear as occasionally happens.

Once, while driving to the hall for a concert, I comforted myself that my thirty minute concerto would be over sooner than the ordeal of pregnant women on their way to the maternity hospital – and much less painful!

I take along an electric massager to particularly demanding concerts and find that a back stage buzz on the neck, shoulders, fingers and relevant pressure points works wonders.

Coping with the minutes before the performance

Experienced performers realise that the anticipation is usually far worse than the event. Many performers find that once they are on-stage, the butterflies simply fly away. They then appear so comfortable and natural in the limelight that their audiences would be amazed to hear of nerves.

Pavarotti describes how his nerves build with a fury when he is backstage waiting, his make-up complete:

Now is the worst time. You have done everything you must do, but there are still twenty minutes before curtain time. Now, you must only sit and wonder how you ever got into this profession where you, a grown man, must get yourself dressed up in a funny costume, walk out onto a stage before thousands of people who may or may not wish you well, and risk making a complete fool of yourself or causing an artistic scandal ...

As the curtain time approaches, lyric opera ceases to be an incredibly rich, tradition-laden treasure house of great art and becomes a minefield of potential disasters ... These are the very worst moments. There is no turning back now. The performance is starting. I sit there with sweat rolling down my neck and I still have three hours to go. I would rather be in any other profession ... I pray ...

I know from the many past performances that I am blessed with a quality which helps me, when the moment is upon me, to shed those paralysing nerves. As the time approaches when I must make my entrance, something clicks in my mind. I become the character and everything else leaves my head.

(My Own Story, Luciano Pavarotti, pp.199-203)

We can be encouraged that top performers suffer such insecurities, just as we do. As they have learned to manage those agonising minutes backstage, so too can we. There are many ways to minimise the panic and to channel our energy and adrenaline into positive directions.

It is important to realise that frantically ploughing through the worrying passages at breakneck speed backstage will probably cause more damage than benefit. To walk on stage knowing that you have just ravelled it up like spaghetti is not confidence-building. Rehearse the dreaded passage if you must ... but at half-speed. Better still, warm up with breathing and stretching exercises, vocal warm-ups, long notes, slow scales.

Warm up with gentle exercises

Warm your hands and fingers by relaxed movements or other gentle exercise. Limber up as athletes do, starting with easy, relaxed actions, then increase the challenge as your muscles loosen up. Water and heat are excellent therapies.

Cold contracts muscles, causing tension. Remember how reluctantly limbs move when we play in draughty halls in winter?

When performing in northern Sweden, often above the Arctic Circle, I learned to thaw my cold fingers under the dressing-room hot taps, the warmth relaxing my muscles. Alternatively, bring gloves or a hot-water bottle.

Turn the fidgets to good use

Waiting backstage, many feel the urge to fidget. Perhaps we should adopt the Mediterranean habit of fiddling with worry-beads – a more healthy distraction than a cigarette.

One of my students found the finger exercises I gave her to develop coordination were even more valuable before a performance, as they forced her to concentrate on something other than her butterflies. (Press each finger against the thumb in turn, first looking, then with eyes closed. Begin with each hand separately, then both together.) Chinese metal balls can be swapped between hands to improve concentration and coordination. Exercise putty balls (bought from a chemist) strengthen as well as exercise hands.

Many find that connecting fingertips (thumb to index finger) helps to centre thoughts and emotions. Kinesthetic 'crossing-over' exercises for the right and left sides of the brain, such as crawling, cross-marching or drawing figures of eights in wide sweeps of the arms not only enable whole-brain function, but get the blood circulating.

Think positively

An important part of your last-minute warm-up is the mental rehearsal. Think through the part you will play, seeing yourself relaxed and successful, tone projecting effortlessly and clearly. Feel the actual touch of the notes under your fingers, your breath warm and easy, flowing smoothly.

Think positive thoughts, while massaging gently above each eye, halfway between your hairline and eyebrows. According to Dennison's Brain Gym, these points are neurological balance points for the stomach meridian. Holding these points releases emotional stress, which you often feel as a queasy stomach, and relaxes your reflexes to act without thinking when under stress. (*Teacher's Edition*, p. 32)

Protect your space

With tensions running high backstage, it's easy to become tangled in other people's traumas. During preparation, we all need space for centring energies, calming thoughts and for mental preparation.

Everyone develops their own personal rituals of preparation. Just as we hope others will respect our space before we launch out into the footlights, so we must be considerate of their need for privacy, even in crowded dressing rooms. Save unnecessary gossip and trivial verbal diarrhoea for the unwinding process later on.

Some use joke-telling as a means of letting off tension and taking their minds off phobias, whereas others flinch from them. Conductor André Previn told how he and the violinist Itzhak Perlman played little games to keep nerves at bay while waiting backstage to perform: they played or whistled movie theme songs for each other to recognise. (*Conductors in Conversation*, Jeannine Wagar, p. 210)

Keep sensitive antennae open for signs that such ploys are not appreciated. Conductor Simone Young says, 'I like to stay on a very business-like level backstage before a performance. And then I'm fine. But I'm liable to completely disintegrate if close friends or family come to wish me luck – they know not to.'

Melbourne conductor David Kram says:

Seek solitude in crowds, depending on your disposition. I like to study the score in the green room rather than my dressing room ... Experience is so effervescent. If you feel out-of-sorts two minutes before curtain-up, it doesn't mean you will feel that way two minutes later. Keep breathing. Keep breathing. Keep breathing.

Last-minute preparations

String players can prepare with long, slow-bowed notes and slow scales, while concentrating on breathing: inhale on the up bow, breathing out on the down bow and bending the knees while exhaling. All wind instrumentalists benefit from playing long, slow notes.

Brass players begin by buzzing on the mouthpiece for a few seconds, before playing long notes in the lower register, gradually working higher. The advantage of starting with the lower notes is that the player gets the feel of attack, lip vibration and breath support without straining.

Singers learn vocal exercises from their teachers. Some of the following more general ideas for actors and singers may be of use to all performers:

Deep breathing is a help to all performers in steadying nerves. The following technique reduces the likelihood of 'overbreathing': Breathe in once (a warm breath). Breathe out twice. (The first will be a warm breath, the second a cool.) Bend forward. Breathe in with arms upraised above your head. Expel the air forcefully in a long, hissing breath while contracting your abdomen muscles.

'Buzz' your lips while singing simple intervals, scales or arpeggios.

Hiss. Expel the air in a long hissing action until your lungs feel quite empty. Your next breath will be easy and natural. This action is useful for getting in touch with the correct mechanism of breathing, noting the action of the muscles of the diaphragm and the lower back, rather than for your actual singing. (See Chapter 8.)

Steeple the hands with fingers pressed together. Breathe deeply through the nose, while pressing the tongue firmly but without strain on the roof of the mouth. You should feel the expansion of the diaphragm as you do so. Release the tongue and exhale through the mouth. Steepling fingers is very beneficial: having your fingertips touching balances and connects the two brain hemispheres. It also softens the muscles along the arm.

Suggestions for the launching pad

Pilots and astronauts vouch that the success of a flight depends enormously on a smooth take-off. Those moments before launching into a performance are crucial in determining whether the performer maintains calm control or succumbs to blind panic. We need to learn to slow down while still on the launching pad, to resist the impulse to rush on and tumble headlong into an incoherent presentation.

From the following suggestions, assemble your own launching pad 'checklist' routine:

- **Sit quietly in your chair backstage in the last minutes, going through slow breathing, energising and centring exercises of your preference.**
- **Give your hands about twenty vigorous shakes so the blood runs to the fingers.**
- **Imagine yourself into the posture, positive mood and shape of an inspiring character.**

A singer, for example, might take on the character of Pavarotti or Cecilia Bartole or Renee Fleming; a violinist, Anne-Sophie Mutter. Assume a confident, smiling celebrity mood. I feel fine, my fingers and shoulders are relaxed, I'm in good form. The audience will enjoy me and applaud wholeheartedly.

- **Make up a body checklist that most effectively highlights the parts of your body which may need relaxation:**

My head feels relaxed, my forehead is smooth, my mouth is easy, not too dry, my neck feels free, my shoulders are low and relaxed, my hands feel free and loose, my chest is upright and full of as much air as I need, my stomach feels comfortable, my legs can carry me easily, my knees are unlocked, my feet can take my weight securely, my toes are unscrunched.

- **Place both feet on the floor and very slowly lean the weight onto them to rise. Standing, check your posture is upright without being rigid. Breathe slowly, deeply.**
- **Paste onto your face either a bright 'I-am-ze-greatest' smile or, if you prefer, a dignified expression.**

'One minute, ladies and gentlemen,' calls the stage manager.

'Good luck, break a leg!' call your colleagues. Or, as the French say, 'Merde'.

Take another deep breath. It's time.

You're on.

55

Summary

Long-term preparation includes:

• Plan: begin the practice program early.

• Slow practice, which allows maximum relaxation and absorption.

• Silent practice, or saying aloud while fingering, secures notes in initial stages.

• Practise in bite-sized bits, teasing the brain with a variety of methods.

Short-term preparation includes:

• Conserve your energy.

• Warm up fingers, voice and lips slowly with long notes, slow scales.

• Protect your space.

• Breathe deeply – the basis of life, energy and relaxation.

• While poised on the launching-pad before walking on stage, progressively relax each section of the body.

How to perform to the best of your ability

I cannot imagine being lackadaisical about a performance.
I treat each encounter as a matter of life and death. The
one important thing I have learnt over the years is the
difference between taking one's work seriously and taking
oneself seriously. The first is imperative and the second is
disastrous.

Ballerina Margot Fonteyn

YOU'RE ON! WALKING ON STAGE as distinct from preparing for it has its own terrors. Singer Grahame McIntosh describes these moments:

Suddenly, the light on the stage manager's desk goes on and you
know for sure that there is no escape. A faintness seems to be
coming over the whole body.

A voice from a hundred kilometres away has just said, 'Ready.'
The legs show signs of paralysis and you need to pay a visit.
That's ridiculous; you've just been.

Hearing a loud burst of applause, your eyes suddenly open in
horror. Your eyes begin to focus and you realise that you are
halfway onto a large brightly lit stage, without even realising that
you have moved. You stop at the grand piano, thinking 'What a
mistake', and look into the wide open spaces. There you see a
veritable sea of white faces leering at you … Go for it! You've
nothing to lose … apart from a career, that is. You drape your
hand over the edge of the piano, in a Rowan Atkinson fashion,
desperately trying to look relaxed. The realisation comes to you
that if you relax too much, you will fold up like a pack of cards.

Smile, that's the shot. Smile at the so-and-sos. But nothing
happens. The paralysis has spread from your legs to your mouth.

57

*A tremendous effort produces a convulsive twitching of your lips.
The idiot complex sets in, so you revert to the hundred per cent
tension. At least, rigor mortis keeps you upright.*

*The pianist, tired of waiting, begins the introduction. This is it.
This is what you have been training for all this time. You prise
open the dry throat, in order to make a sound like the last rose of
summer, and what comes out is more like the first rasp of winter.*

It can require enormous courage to walk on stage and perform. To
manage this while projecting poise and conviction, let us take up the
routine established at the end of the previous chapter.

Perhaps your stomach is an aviary of butterflies and moths. A
compost heap of worms, caterpillars and other greeblies are gnawing
your gut. But somehow, before walking on-stage, you must attach a
bright smile onto your face. People do respond to a positive face and
especially to a smile. However, if your personality prefers a more
sober, dignified mien, this is also acceptable. Be yourself. To think
positively, take singer Beverley McCarthy's advice: 'I walk on as if I
just sang the piece and this is the encore.'

Stage presentation

Stand upright, but not ramrod stiff, with shoulders down and chin
slightly raised as if looking over the crowd. Walk confidently, but not
too fast, onto the stage.

Ah, you hear the applause? Remember, it is basic good manners to
acknowledge this with a smile and a bow. If the audience claps and
you ignore their gesture, this says tacitly that you don't think much of
their judgment. (Orchestral players and choristers are the exception:
the conductor bows on their behalf.)

Please don't curtsy! Unless you are the prima donna of the opera,
ballet or show, this is definitely passé. On the other hand, a reluctant
jerk of the head implies, 'My teacher says I have to bow; well, this
will do.' A bow should be slow; look down at your shoes, while
(gracefully) elevating your posterior – think 'hippopotamus' or 'I am
ze greatest' – then return to standing position.

Practise stage deportment before the big day, with a mirror or
video camera and the feedback of a teacher or colleague. Stage

presentation is often forgotten or underrated, but professional poise can be as memorable as the content of your performance.

Unconsciously, people assess you just as much by your manner and body language as by the actual performance. Research has shown that audiences tend to focus on the 'right-hemisphere brain' aspects like body language, rhythm and imagery more than on actual words, and that fifty-five per cent of your presentation's impact derives from your posture, gestures and eye contact. Voice tone and inflection determines thirty-eight per cent and only seven per cent the actual content!

Body language tells all

When adjudicating competitions, I can usually predict a good or a poor performance before a note has been played, because body language reveals confidence or lack of it. The tenor who slinks furtively on-stage, obviously wishing he were elsewhere, should expand his chest out confidently, pretending to be Pavarotti. The pianist who sits with shoulders protectively hunched around her, hiding behind her hair, invariably plays with a thin, mousey sound and mistakes reveal lack of preparation. If our body language says, 'Listen to me: I am the greatest!' a large proportion of the audience is prepared to believe us.

Dress is important

Its importance lies not just in how it looks to others, but because it increases our own confidence, poise and positive anticipation. Generally in music performances, it is preferable to err on the side of overdress than under, if only for our own confidence. On the other hand, one needs to be aware of fashion trends. There can be a significant difference between an ankle or floor-length dress.

High-profile women are continually pressured by the vagaries of fickle fashion. They feel compelled to present themselves well, but the cost of a new evening dress may exceed the performance fee. One solution, invaluable to television presenters and soloists, is to buy designer labels at pre-loved boutiques for a fraction of their original cost. Justify it as saving resources. Barbra Streisand and violinist Nigel Kennedy built whole personas out of thrift shop gear.

Taffeta may be popular in retro shops, but it is not advisable for performance, as pianist Elizabeth Smart discovered: 'When I was a young girl of fifteen, my only concert dress was made from then-fashionable rustly taffeta. Unfortunately, when performing my knees shook and the dress rattled.'

Above all, dress comfortably in a manner that enhances and expresses your personality. It is a sad truth that society does judge by outward appearances. If we look like somebody important or glamorous, the audience is more inclined to take us seriously. One specific aspect of overdressing to avoid is wearing excessively high-heeled shoes. Glamorous as they may look, these can cause foot cramps, as well as upsetting your posture. An exception to this is Simone Young, who conducts whole Wagner opera cycles in high heels – her early ballet training has accustomed her to the height.

Check new shoes for slippery soles and take the precaution of rubbing them over a rough surface like cement to avoid an experience of a lead tenor in *La Traviata*; rushing in to the passionate reunion at Violetta's deathbed, he skidded and arrived flat on his back under the bed. The soprano sang bravely on as if nothing had happened.

Women should bring a spare pair of stockings – two if wearing black hose which inexplicably ladder more often! Check for hanging petticoats before going on-stage. Men should always check that flies are securely zipped, as these two salutary tales should indicate:

At an orchestral concert, I saw the principal violist, who was prone to flamboyant bow strokes and gestures, suddenly notice that his fly was unzipped. He simply placed his viola on his knees, re-zipped the fly and proceeded.

Then there is a story, perhaps apocryphal, of a conductor who came on stage, bowed to the audience and then to the orchestra. Realising in horror that his fly was undone, he hastily turned his back on his orchestral colleagues …

Dress must be appropriate to the occasion. Female cellists should wear slacks or a full skirt, not a mini-skirt!

Do check suitability of dress with management or other colleagues, so colours and styles blend. I learned this lesson early in my career:

While still a university student, I freelanced with my first professional orchestra. This particular week I was booked for a Sunday afternoon concert in the Botanic Gardens, but was not needed for the more glamorous Saturday night promenade. The inebriated orchestral manager attached himself to my arm and leered at me: 'Don't forget, wear something bright, eh?' But surely the Gardens concerts were black-and-white affairs? Perhaps their image had been upgraded.

Being inexperienced, it never occurred to me to check: the orchestral manager knew the schedule, surely. I bought a long, bright red dress for the occasion ... and spent the whole concert skulking behind the music stand, my face as red as my dress.

Prepare and pack all clothes well before the event. I have sabotaged pre-concert calm with a scorch mark on my dress and wasted warm-up time fabricating a bow to cover it.

Take your time

Take a few moments to poise yourself before starting. These seconds may seem an age to you, but they are not to the audience. They capture the audience's attention and the atmosphere's spell, quieten the rowdy and establish a calm beginning for yourself. Silence is a potent attention-gatherer.

A positive opening is crucial

The first notes or words are very important for your own confidence and the audience's appraisal of you. If your initial sound is squeezed out with strangled tension or a miscalculated projection, your stomach will plummet. You will think, 'Oh no, this is going to be a fiasco!'

On the other hand, if that first note or word sings out beautifully modulated with seemingly effortless ease, your confidence will soar with it. First impressions linger in listeners' appraisals. In most auditions, a few seconds are enough to tell the panel if they are interested in the applicant.

When I adjudicate, I notice constantly that a player's control of their first note or lack of it is usually indicative of their whole performance. On the other hand, if you suffer an initial mishap, don't give up. Many players warm into their presentations.

Establish contact with the audience

As you walk on stage, remind yourself that most of the audience is probably there to enjoy themselves, to be enlightened, touched, or relaxed by what you are offering. They are not necessarily there to criticise. They want you to succeed.

Temporarily adopt a friendly face from the audience and pretend she is your grandmother in whose eyes you can do no wrong – and play for her.

Train yourself to lift your eyes from the floor, a giveaway sign of insecurity. Many nervous performers try to pretend that the audience is not really there, fixing their gaze on inanimate objects like the ceiling or a light fitting. This alienates the listeners and gives the performer a glassy, unnatural bearing. The public does respond to eye contact. Some singers worry about forgetting words if they actually look at the audience, so they focus just a little above their faces, creating the same personal effect.

It is far better to cultivate an attitude of giving to the audience, rather than trying to pretend they have been magically spirited away. Audiences notice and appreciate this and respond in turn.

Consider: what is our relationship with the audience? What are we trying to do to them or for them? As performers we try to:

- **Give the audience enjoyment, humour, release from
the mundane routines of life, respite and escape from
various situations. In those special moments, we
share our deeper feelings and thoughts with them.**

- **Express the author or composer's voice and interpret
his or her ideas, moods, songs, emotions, messages of
humanity, life, light and beauty. We have a sacred
trust to interpret the author or composer's intentions
as best we can. In becoming one with the
composition, we are honoured to share in the genius
of a great composer.**

- **Communicate and share an understanding of the**

variety of colours, moods and emotions in the music, play or dance (love, beauty, joy, anguish, sadness, triumph, pain, etcetera.).

• **Share your understanding of form, structure and sounds.**

For some, there may be a need to display the dazzling techniques perfected through hours of toil. How many listeners really come in order to be stunned by pyrotechnics? Often the goal of impressing people becomes a burden. How many in the audience want to compare us with the last performance they heard of that concerto? Perhaps a small minority, but what of the majority who just hope to enjoy themselves, to replenish their spirit and soul, or to escape from the drudgery of the past week? What of the snuggling couple out for a romantic evening? Play for them.

Organist Gillian Weir agrees with this:

Remember the audience are there because they want a pleasant evening with marvellous music. They are not there to find fault and criticise. If there are some critical people, who you imagine want you to go wrong, then the odd wrong note here or there will make them happy, so you will have pleased somebody even then!

(Kate Jones, *Stage Fright? It'll be All Right on the Night*,
BBC Music Magazine, June 2001, p. 42)

Never underestimate an audience or look down on them. Even when we play at a small-town affair to a supposedly lacklustre crowd, invariably one person later floors us with knowledgeable comments. Even if we think the wedding guests are too busy drinking and joking to listen, some do appreciate our soulful arrangements. A string quartet busked in the same Parisian Metro beat over a long weekend. They were a little unnerved when one regular listener brought along the musical scores to better enjoy the performance!

Establish audience contact by giving to your listeners. Absorb yourself in projecting the music, enjoy yourself.

Claudio Arrau sums it up this way:

You should always project on an audience; you should never play just for yourself. But your first aim should not be to try to please the audience. You should give them what you have to give – the

message of the composer through your own personality. It is
always the composer's intentions and the deeper meaning of the
work that counts most, not whether or not the performance pleases
... you should develop resistance against following the commercial
trends in interpretation. Commerce and art are two different roads.
(Pianists at Play, Dean Elder, p. 45)

Encourage supportive friends and family to attend your performances. Empathy from caring, understanding supporters makes a huge difference to our ability to project, communicate and, consequently, to relax and perform at our best.

Certainly, I have found a crowd of supporters has helped me. I was to play in an unpublicised final examination performance to four intimidating examiners writing busily in an otherwise empty auditorium. Realising this would send more jitters than usual skittering through my system, I rallied a roomful of friends, family and students to attend. Their positive empathy counteracted any negative currents and blocked my vision of the examiners' assessing expressions.

The support and encouragement from a friendly audience can improve one's confidence enormously. I encountered a very pleasant custom in Sweden. People come up after a performance, shake your hand and say, 'Tack für konsert' – 'Thanks for the concert'. Never mind whether you stumbled, that you botched the semiquavers or squeaked throughout. You gave something of yourself, made an effort – and they appreciate that. Even better, when we see similar support from colleagues. At a recent performance of the Moscow Radio Orchestra, I was impressed that the players shook hands with each other while still on-stage.

Imagine the empathetic waves if we all propagated this supportive attitude to performance! Haven't we often hesitated to go backstage and congratulate a player, trying to formulate some clever, perceptive pronouncement? Why do we need to make any judgment? Isn't it enough that we appreciated and enjoyed their contribution? Just thank them for that.

Focus your attention on an encouraging friend or supportive

relative and play to that person. Drag your eyes away from that threatening rival who fidgets with the score in the front row.

If you see a familiar face frowning in the audience, have the courage to assume that it's caused by his poor indigestion, toothache, a fight with their partner, or today's fax from the bank manager – not by your own performance.

At this point, it is useful to consider the Ten Commandments for audiences, so that we don't distract those who perform for us:

- **Latecomers shall only enter – quietly – between movements or pieces.**
- **Thou shalt not talk to thy neighbour during the concert.**
- **Thou shalt turn off thy mobile phone.**
- **Thou shalt not sit in the front row solemnly studying the score.**
- **If thou really must cough, thou shalt hide thy head in thy handbag and exit fast.**
- **If thou hast 'flu, stay home and recover in bed. (At least, bring cough lozenges.)**
- **Thou shalt remove babies who cry. (Many the concert halls I have circumnavigated with prams, after my children tired of their cultural experiences.)**
- **Thou shalt not undermine performers during the interval with neatly placed barbs.**
- **Thou shalt not click cameras during performances, especially when accompanied by a flash.**
- **Thou shalt not tap thy toe in syncopation to the beat – which is a polite way of saying, out of time.**

During the performance

Be prepared for the flow of adrenaline and welcome it, for it will give energy and strength to your performances, but don't become obsessed about it. Remember, it is a natural, normal and helpful reaction so long as you don't fight it.

Learn to handle mistakes in a performance

What to do when you make a mistake? The first rule is to keep going! That moment is already passed; you cannot go back in time and fix it. It is overlaid with the beautiful sounds and phrases, or the intelligent content of your speech.

Don't let any fluster over small mishaps drag down the rest of your performance; put them behind you. Don't look back – or, like Lot's wife, you will be turned into a pillar of salt, or something that tastes equally bitter.

Remember, any mishaps are your secret. Don't move a muscle, flinch, pull faces, or in any other way wave a big placard announcing: 'Oops, I boo-booed!'

If you do make a mistake, flinching visibly will only give ammunition to your possible critics. Why draw attention to something they might otherwise have missed? Perhaps they were daydreaming in that alpha state that music induces, not hanging on your every note. Probably, most don't really know the score intimately. Even if they do, it is possible your mistake was not as obvious as you thought. They might just think you added an enterprising ad lib or ornament.

It's surprising how, even if we have played a piece many times ourselves, we hear it from a different perspective when sitting in the audience. Many people miss small mistakes unless they have a photographic memory. If you can't keep a poker face after a mistake, at least throw it off with a slight smile instead of a grimace.

Turn negatives into positives

Revel in the challenge of extricating yourself, as did Franz Liszt. A contemporary, Amy Fay, recalled that Liszt often played handfuls of wrong notes in his improvisations, but it did not trouble him in the least: 'On the contrary, he rather enjoys it … it always amuses him when he comes down squarely wrong.' It gave him the opportunity to display his ingenuity in extricating himself through new and unexpected beauties. (*Success in Music and How it is Won*, Henry T. Fink, p. 291)

She described how:

He was rolling up the piano in arpeggios in a very grand manner indeed, when he struck a half-tone short of the high note on which

he intended to end … a half smile came over his face as if to say,
'Don't fancy that this little thing disturbs me' and he instantly went
meandering down the piano in harmony with the false note … and
then rolled deliberately up in a second grand sweep, this time
striking true … Instead of giving you a chance to say, 'He has
made a mistake', he forced you to say, 'He has shown us how to
get out of a mistake.'

(*The Great Pianists*, Harold C. Schonberg, p. 167)

How much does it matter that Mendelssohn criticised Liszt for 'such a pitiably imperfect style, so uncleanly, so ignorantly' with wrong harmonies and lamentable misdemeanours? Yet his reputation has endured as a remarkable pianist. The person who has never made a mistake has never made anything!

Another disarming tactic is to be open and honest with the audience. The conductor Hans Richter once threw his orchestra into momentary confusion with incorrect cues during Brahms' *Academic Festival Overture*. He repeated the work, then turned around to explain to the audience that the fault was his, not the orchestra's.

We have all heard versions of the saying: 'If I play a mistake, the audience remembers it for five seconds, my teacher remembers for five days, and I remember it for five years.' A few wrong notes do not negate the positive aspects of your performance. It was said of Rubenstein that on occasion he dropped more notes than he played. But with what exquisite touch, what sensitive feeling!

In fact, the ancient Greeks believed that it was necessary to include some small imperfections in their otherwise superbly proportioned architecture or art. Otherwise, they might offend the gods by striving for perfection … yet they came as close to it as anyone.

We can learn from our mistakes, so repeat performances of hazardous pieces are invaluable. Take every possible chance to perform. Fabricate even more. The important part of improving is not to play the perfect performance, but learning how to get out of a mistake. Turn it to positive advantage; be encouraged and strengthened for the next performance.

Strive for excellence, rather than perfection, and the audience may so enjoy your beautiful, expressive tone that they will readily forgive a few stray notes.

Soloists, especially singers, who have greater opportunities for communication with the audience than orchestral players, can make the mistake part of the performance.

Peter Egan, Sydney singer and speaker, turns such negative mishaps to positive use by audibly asking the accompanist, 'What's the next word?' By turning it into a joke and by revealing this fallible, human aspect, he immediately gets his audience on-side. They respond generously to such admissions, risky as they may seem, for people like to know we are human. Thus he endears himself to his audience.

Learn to handle memory loss

Memory lapses, or 'drying', can happen to anyone. If you don't make a 'thing' about it, the audience will either not notice or will forgive. They may be relaxed in an alpha state of relaxation and most won't even notice mishaps that seem enormous in the performer's eyes. Singers may feel safer with small cue cards in a pocket, even if they don't refer to them.

The great guitarist Segovia performed in London at the age of ninety. When he lost his place in a Bach fugue, he simply said 'Excuse me' and went back to the beginning. Surely, no one in the auditorium held it against him.

Singer Kathryn Sadler advises:

A secure memorisation process begins with the first impressions while learning the piece. Write out English texts in a little note book and refer to them in any free moments. Research the exact meaning of obscure poems. This helps the memory and also adds depths to interpretation. Practise telling the story of 'long story' songs in extemporised prose so that the order of events is clear; underline key words in each verse that will trigger that order.

'List' songs, where each line is an entity in itself and has no recognisable connection with that which precedes or follows, simply have to be learned 'parrot fashion'.

With foreign language texts, write the exact word for word translation over the original lines. Regardless of the language, no

performer is truly ready to perform until the text, including those
in foreign languages, can be recited with dramatic integrity
without the melody to help. Once this is done, the music serves to
tie up the memorisation parcel.

If we do not feel totally secure in our memorisation, why not try a compromise? Place the music reassuringly on the music stand, but begin performing from memory, edging closer if necessary. Pianists may gain confidence just knowing that the closed score is there in front of them.

Memorisation is a useful tool towards a more confident, focused performance. However, many excellent musicians may avoid performance because of insecure memory. Audiences are deprived of a wealth of wonderful music which is rarely heard merely because it is too difficult to be safely memorised. What a waste! Surely, the expectation of memorising increasingly difficult works has created a huge burden for our performers! This has increased performance anxiety for many, stunting their ability to perform to their full potential.

Pianist Adolf Henselt drew rave notices from Robert Schumann and Liszt for the subtlety yet strength of his fingers. He became a compulsive practiser, working ten hours a day – even with a dummy keyboard while travelling – and a terrifyingly perfectionist teacher. His pathological terror of the public probably originated when he was so embarrassed by a memory lapse at his debut that he left the stage and refused to return.

How much insecurity is caused by the great god of memorisation! Even if many performers do manage the correct notes, how often is the price a less expressive, more reserved and careful performance? If Rubenstein had used music, he might have been spared the torments of stage fright in his later years. Do we need to bow to this god?

Pianist Myra Hess took a stand against the shibboleth of memorisation. She made a point of playing at least one work per concert with the music before her.

Competitors have been eliminated from competitions because of memory lapse. Are such competitions a survival of the fittest – or the best memory?

The perspective changes if we realise that memorisation is a relatively recent expectation. Clara Schumann was the first pianist to play from memory in 1837, a feat her peers dismissed as 'insufferable … pretentious'. Even years after, it was considered bad form and disrespectful to play the music of a master without the score. Yet, when elderly, Schumann did use the music, even for concertos that she knew thoroughly. The other leader of the memorisation fashion was Franz Liszt: it suited him to dispense with the music because his pieces were largely improvised.

These two pianists also paved the way for the now accepted single-performer concerts. Previously, programs were balanced with many varied instruments and players. Before the 1830s, a featured artist was only expected to perform two or three pieces. Surely this practice needs a new vogue. Would not a whole evening of unremitting solo piano or soprano or violin be enhanced if all three shared the program? Today's performers face the extra challenge to maintain concentration, both their own and that of the audience, for a whole concert.

However, this argument does not negate the value of memorisation. Singers will need to learn their words if they are acting, or moving about on-stage. Many performers feel more rather than less free when they play from memory. But those who choose to loosen the memorisation noose in certain circumstances should do so without apology or guilt.

Curb excess body movement

My natural inclination is to move freely while playing. When video-taped as a student I was more off the screen than on it. Now I try to curb excess movement in slow pieces particularly, as it may distract from the mood and distort the sound. Those sensitive feelings we think we express may be merely acted out, with the intention channelled into our body movements rather than into the actual sound. Unnecessary movement can be disconcerting to the audience.

Too much bodily movement is often a compensation for inadequate ability:

When I see a pianist waving about in the slow movement, staring
up into the air, I wonder what is the matter with him. He is looking

for a fly on the ceiling, perhaps? You notice in the last movement
he only has time to look at the keys!'
(*Virtuoso: The Story of John Ogden*, Brenda Ogden & Michael Kerr, p. 131)

Talk to the audience

Whenever appropriate, my husband, Antoni, and I introduce performances with a few words about the pieces, perhaps using a humorous story relating to their background. This considerably warms the audience, who find it reassuring that musicians have voices as well – it makes us more human. Where relevant, humour can be a big audience winner, adding to the enjoyment of the concert. We are entertainers, after all.

I learned the value of this when performing chamber music concerts in Sweden. A friend said, 'The music is fine, but why don't you talk to us?' – 'What, in Swedish? With poor grammar, mistakes?' – 'That doesn't matter. Please, talk to us.' Toni and I found that people warmed to us because we showed ourselves as human and fallible.

In fact, people appreciate a performer's willingness to reveal some weaknesses. It can be liberating to make a fool of ourselves without qualms, not caring what people think of us!

Speaking directly to the audience is only possible for musicians in chamber music or solo situations. No one would appreciate the third trombonist's impromptu exposition in an orchestral concert. And a degree of formality is still expected of concerto soloists. However, the popularity of pre-concert talks shows that audiences appreciate hearing information relevant to the concert. How much more intimate if it comes from the artists themselves.

Take action if you feel ill

If the feeling of illness comes before the performance, apply cold packs to the back or take a cold shower if you are hot and sweaty. Homoeopathic remedies include gelsemium, especially effective for stomach nerves in stage fright situations and for 'flu. Very dilute homeopathic aconite eases effects of fear, fright and anxiety. The Dr Bach drops called Rescue Remedy are used by many stage fright sufferers. These are available at health shops and some chemists or through a naturopath.

Many fear the sheer stamina required to stand, poised, for hours on end. Conductors and choristers may be on their feet for long periods. For example, Handel's *Messiah* is a massive work. What to do if you feel faint in the middle of the *Hallelujah Chorus*? It is better to unobtrusively sit down and lower your head as soon as faintness threatens, rather than to struggle on and risk making an exhibition of yourself by landing on the floor.

It is difficult to concentrate when standing for long periods, so a comfortable balance on the feet is essential. Resist the temptation to glamorise your appearance by wearing high heels. Wear a flatter shoe which provides comfort and stability. Avoid tight clothes which restrict easy breathing.

Stand with an upright posture, but not rigidly, and allow your arms and hands to hang loosely by your side. Faintness is caused by lack of blood circulation. You can counteract this by many subtle means: wiggle your toes and move your hands and head unobtrusively.

If you suffer a nosebleed on-stage, press your finger on the indentation of your nose. This cuts off the blood supply. Press firmly for three minutes. As the adrenaline rush causes blood to pump faster, it is not unusual for capillaries to burst, which causes a nosebleed. If an ice-pack is available back-stage, press or place it on the bridge of the nose, just between the eyebrows. Tilt your head back slightly and gently squeeze your nostrils. You can also press or massage the bumps at the back of your head where it joins to your neck. An old folk remedy for nosebleeds is to soak lemon juice onto cotton wool and press it to the nostril. Powdered tea was once used as a snuff to stop nosebleeds, as was dried witch-hazel.

Peppermint has been used as a heart tonic to relieve palpitations and as a relaxant for such conditions as indigestion, migraine, headache, nausea and travel sickness. Peppermint oil was used as an inhalant during fainting fits and dizziness and as a gargle for sore throats.

Organise to avoid embarrassment

Many calamities can be avoided by careful pre-concert organisation. Allow time beforehand to organise lighting, space and rickety music stands. Stories are legion of dire moments resulting from these aspects.

Cellist Rosemary Quinn tells us:

I was playing in the Australian Chamber Orchestra at the Sydney Opera House before thousands of people. Just at the end of a symphony, my music stand gracefully folded over, depositing the folder of music in my lap. Fortunately, I managed to improvise the dominant-tonic chords until the final cadence.

Unfamiliar venues may present unexpected hazards, as I discovered. While touring northern Sweden with Mozart's opera *The Marriage of Figaro*, I gained a dubious show-stopping reputation in a small township north of the Arctic Circle. We performed in a hall so small that the players were cramped into the orchestra pit like sardines. I did not realise that a well-stacked power-point under my chair lit the whole stage and the musicians' music stands ... until I moved a few millimetres and blacked out the whole performance.

It is important to double-check that all music parts are present and intact before the performance, taping any additions or photocopied page-turns so they do not disappear at crucial moments.

At the end of the performance

At the conclusion, whatever the mishaps, they are behind you. Don't rush from the platform. Wait a few moments for the listeners to savour the magic, unbroken by the shuffling of pages and equipment.

No matter how many mistakes are indelibly etched in your memory, come up smiling. It is important to develop acting skills so you can flash a toothy 'I-am-still-ze-greatest!' smile at the audience. Many less critical people will be happy to believe you. Project the expectation that the audience will clap.

The performance is not over with the last note. A poised, professional bow is part of the act, however brilliantly or badly you played. Less experienced players rush offstage to hide their faces, but a slow, dignified acknowledgement of the applause helps to rescue an unfavourable impression.

Even now, when the strain is over, take care, don't rush.

Pity one poor cellist who took a bow after his concerto. He fell on to his centuries-old Italian master-crafted instrument, smashing it to pieces.

Whatever disasters befall us, we have to pick ourselves up with some grace, bow and muster courage to go back on stage again. Whatever our own ghastly memories of embarrassments in public performance, surely performers have experienced much worse!

Summary

- **Practise stage presentation beforehand. Graciously acknowledge applause with a bow – both at the beginning and the end.**

- **Take a few moments to poise before launching out; a securely produced first sound is important both for the audience's first impression and to lift the performer's spirits.**

- **More listeners are present to enjoy your performance than to criticise. When you feel particularly insecure, encourage positive supporters to attend.**

- **Check all aspects of equipment and dress beforehand to avoid mishaps.**

- **A few mistakes do not a fiasco make. Put them behind you and keep going, whatever happens.**

How to prepare physically for peak performance

Music – what a noble art, what a terrible profession.
(Hector Berlioz, composer)

It is a wretched trade, being a concert artist. Preferably one ought to make music for oneself and a few friends.
(Joseph Joachim, violin virtuoso)

TOURING SOUNDS SO GLAMOROUS to those who don't have to zoom through six countries in two weeks, seeing little more than the hotel room, auditorium and transit lounge. Long hours on buses, trains or aeroplanes are draining. Add a transport strike, bomb scare or fog-bound airport, and the frustrations and disorientations may become barely endurable. Pianist Bruno Gelber bursts the glamour bubble:

> *This way of life is difficult. Sometimes, I wake up in the middle of the night and – I promise, it's totally true – I don't have any idea where I am. I don't even know which country I'm in. So I sleep with the light on. My dream, which would be exceptional for me, is what would be natural for a normal person – to stay in one place, to watch TV.*

> Shirley Apthorp, *Touching Triumph on the World Stage*,
> The Australian, June 14, 1996, p.11)

Even without jet-lag, travel is exhausting. The body strains to maintain a sense of balance in moving vehicles through compensating motion with the middle ear. Motion also affects binocular vision and depth perception. Neck rolls and the Brain Gym exercises found in Chapter 8 can ease such aspects.

Minimise jet lag by drinking copious amounts of water, resisting alcohol, stretching in the aisles and on fuel stops. Exercise in your seat with shoulder shrugs and toe-circles. Adjust to the new time zone rather than fall straight into bed on arrival.

Adapting to changed time zones and new acoustics in strange halls each night is challenging. Long hours spent reading notes in fluorescent light is tiring; research has found such lighting can discoordinate the two hemispheres of the brain.

We may rub shoulders day and night with abrasive, incompatible people, then struggle home jet-lagged to make up students' missed lessons.

Many freelance players dare not turn down a well paid all-night recording session. Add to this carrying heavy equipment, a string of late night gigs, winding down in a smoky pub with a few drinks, then snatching minimal sleep before a long drive to that out-of-town date next day. Worrying about lack of sleep soon escalates into insomnia.

Fears and life generally seem more daunting when we are overtired or physically depleted. Many performers sink deeper and deeper into such exhaustion that humdrum boredom would seem a luxury! It is not easy to maintain health when hectic schedules invite junk-food and frequent sweetened coffees – but energy levels plummet lower still when the sugar levels drop.

Do you feel slumped, depressed, merely to read of – let alone endure – such rigours? They are very real challenges. However, jazz musician James Morrison sees a different paradigm. His talent extends beyond music to an ability to enjoy his hectic lifestyle, even if it means a return flight Sydney to Berlin for a forty-five minute 'gig'!

I've got myself psyched a different way about flying, 'cos I have to do it so much. People get off international flights and they're exhausted. If someone said to you, 'Here's a reclining armchair, a supply of videos, and we'll bring you food whenever you want it – would you mind just sitting in here for today and tonight?' are you going to feel exhausted at the end of that, or say, 'What a lovely break today – no phones and I didn't have to run around anywhere.' Because you're flying to another country, all of a sudden you think it's exhausting. Now when I get really tired, I think if only I had an international flight I could recuperate.

Jet lag? Morrison dismisses that, partly because a musician's hours are so odd anyway; also, as a pilot himself, he is used to altitude. Again, attitude turns a negative into a positive. Within Australia, he chooses to fly his band to out-of-town gigs in his own plane. Rather than struggle to a mid-morning flight, risking loss or damage of instruments and battling traffic home with most of the day wasted, he reasons that he can sleep the same six hours in his own bed, with the day ahead of him. He says:

> *I love flying and always have ... After playing a gig, sitting up*
> *there above the clouds at 13,000 feet, the glow of the instrument*
> *panel, the stars and the plane cruising along that's so relaxing.*
> *You don't need a break because it's so varied.*
>
> (John Shand, *All Good Fun: The Life and Times*
> *of James Morrison,* Australasian Jazz'n'Blues)

Athletes prepare the whole person – body, mind and spirit – for a big event. Even more, performing artists' stress levels need optimum health through a balanced lifestyle, healthy nutrition, exercise and sufficient sleep. Pianist Paderewski's antidote for nerves and staleness was a few hours of physical field-labour in the sun.

Conductor Herbert Blomstedt has this solution:

> *Without the Sabbath I wouldn't be able to work as much as I do ...*
> *it's a great relief to have a supreme command which says, 'This is*
> *not the day to work. This is the day to recognise God's presence*
> *and to reflect and respond to it.' Without that command I would be*
> *studying scores all the time and would burn myself out.*
>
> (*Conductors in Conversation*, Jeannine Wagar, p. 8)

Getting adequate sleep

> *... the innocent sleep,*
> *Sleep that knits up the ravelled sleaves of care,*
> *The death of each day's life, sore labour's bath,*
> *Balm of hurt minds, great nature's second course,*
> *Chief nourisher in life's feast.*
>
> (Shakespeare: *Macbeth*)

Regular, adequate sleep enables us to perform to the best of our ability. Yet tour organisers usually have to stretch the performers rather than the budget.

People slept an average of nine-and-a-half hours in the days before electricity and videos. These days, seven-and-a-half hours is the average, though one in a hundred manages well on less than five-and-a-half hours. Apparently, the others don't; about one-third of people in the Western world complain of chronic fatigue. This calls for solutions.

Studies have shown that lack of the important phase of sleep known as rapid eye movement (REM) diminishes our memory and absorption of information. Parents who have endured sleepless nights with young children soon realise that lack of sleep reduces to shreds their nerves, objectivity and ability to cope with stressful situations.

Here we are, the night before our big solo or opening night, fretting 'I can't possibly sleep!' A sedative is all too tempting, but non-pharmacological means of promoting sleep are healthier in the long run. Try these techniques instead:

The day's wind-down: Exercise in the afternoon to help the body unwind and so induce better sleep. However, don't exercise too late into the evening as it can temporarily rev you up instead. Get plenty of fresh air. It's important for good health, especially for insomniacs, who tend to breathe shallowly.

The pre-bed wind-down: Keep a regular wake-and-sleep routine. The body's circadian rhythms are disrupted unless we go to bed and rise at roughly the same time each day. If we have poor sleep one night, sleeping in only disrupts the pattern further.

Time your sleep sensibly: Where possible, try to go to bed by 10pm to avail yourself of the slight drop in sugar levels and circadian rhythms.

Develop eating habits that assist the body: A huge meal just before bed requires more energy for digestion and can cause vivid dreams. By eating the main meal at midday and a light evening meal, such as a salad or soup, the body, brain and digestive system are able to relax overnight. Before bed, a light snack which includes calcium, like cheese on toast, aids sleep.

Drink warm milk or herbal tea: Chamomile, valerian or passion flower before bed usually helps. Restrict fluid intake in the afternoon and evening, so you don't wake in the night to trek to the toilet and then have difficulty recapturing sleep.

Wind down the day's tensions: Make some quiet time before heading for bed. Pray, reflect on the day's events, plan the coming activities and resolve any lingering conflicts so that they don't join you in bed.

Release your worries: It's difficult to sleep when the day's events and aggravations race through the mind. Look at each one in turn and say to yourself, 'I release this and am now at peace.'

Use relaxation techniques: Ten minutes of stretching and yoga, exercises like alternative nostril breathing, or 'meditation on a candle' will calm the mind and relax tension. Progressively relax the muscles of your body, starting with your head and moving down. Or tense and relax each muscle group in turn.

Water therapy: Indulge with a soak in a warm bath or jacuzzi. A few drops of lavender in the water is wonderfully relaxing and has been scientifically shown to increase the amount of deep sleep. Even just a footbath with hot water and bath salts will help.

Herbs, essential oils and aromatherapy: Sprinkle a few drops to luxuriously scent the bath, or release relaxing aromas in the bedroom through a vaporiser or oil burner. Of the many possibilities, the following have well-recognised benefits:

- **marjoram is said to be sedating, a muscle relaxant**
- **neroli relieves stress**
- **chamomile soothes an overactive mind**
- **bergamot uplifts anxiety and depression; eases stress, negative thoughts and lack of confidence**
- **orange uplifts and relaxes**
- **lavender soothes and calms. It has been used for centuries to ease nervous states such as stage fright, insomnia, fear (of failure, of the future, of people), insecurity, panic attacks.**

Then, after your bath, lie down on a herb pillow filled with lavender, chamomile, hops and linden blossoms.

Enjoy close encounters of the lovemaking kind: What's more soporific relaxation than cuddling close to a loving partner in a warm, comfortable bed after lovemaking? Research has shown that hormonal mechanisms triggered during sexual activity help to enhance sleep.

Warm your toes: Experienced mothers know that babies sleep better, even in hot climates, if their toes are warm in socks. So, surely, do we. If body heat is not available, warmth is better enhanced by a hot water bottle than electric blankets, which can drain energy.

Soothe the spirit: Relax the mind with beautiful music, perhaps while reading a spiritually uplifting book, praying or meditating.

Think beautiful thoughts: Remember that any worries and negative thoughts taken to bed with you will receive eight hours of undivided attention from your brain. Instead, repeat positive affirmations over and over, such as:

'I am relaxed and coping and doing fine. Tomorrow will be a fruitful and positive day. I can sleep, I feel heavy and relaxed.'

Write out positive thoughts and think them over and over. Make up short, positive 'I' statements in the present tense. Sing them in the shower before bed, set to your own melodies or mould them into a popular tune.

Repeat soothing verses such as 'If you sit down, you will not be afraid; When you lie down, your sleep will be sweet' (*Proverbs* 3: 24); 'I will both lie down and sleep in peace; for you alone, O Lord, make me lie down in safety' (*Psalms* 4: 8); 'For he gives sleep to his beloved' (*Psalms* 127: 2); 'Those of steadfast mind you keep in peace because they trust in you' (*Isaiah* 26: 3).

See yourself achieving your goals, enjoying your work. Envision beauty. While we are sleeping the subconscious mind continues to work on those thoughts we take to bed.

When sleep will not come:

Mentally repeat a simple word over and over and over, the more bland the better, to block other thoughts from racing around your mind. Even more boring than counting sheep!

Choose a movement that signifies closing down the mind for the night. Perhaps you visualise shutters rolling down, or you mentally close curtains, or draw a blind. Repeat this over and over until you really do close down.

Interrupt your thoughts. Break the tyranny of a racing brain by getting up to go to the toilet, to look at the stars or to walk in the garden for a few moments. It sometimes helps to do half an hour's light reading. (Not work. Bed should be a place for glorious relaxing.) Maybe you were just genuinely not tired. Forcing sleep only causes a greater strain.

Count backwards from one hundred, with a slow breath in and out to each count.

Recite something familiar – that Shakespeare sonnet you learned in high school, the Creed or 23rd Psalm. Bore yourself to sleep by reciting French verbs or Latin conjugations.

Have a massage. Persuade a partner or friend to do this or pay a professional to massage you, especially your neck, shoulders and feet.

Try acupuncture – it can help insomniacs.

Use magnesium phosphate supplements – they help to sedate and relax the central nervous system. Also helpful is potassium phosphate. Check dosage with your alternative or medical practitioner.

A medical practitioner can prescribe Tryptophan, a nutrient supplement which is converted in the brain to a chemical called 'serotonin'. This controls sleep, appetite, libido and moods. If stress has depleted stores of Vitamin B6 in the body, absorption of Tryptophan is less efficient. However, excessive Vitamin B6 can cause bad dreams.

Homoeopathic drops like Gelsemium relax and aid migraine sufferers.

Try a video rewind. Rudolf Steiner suggested a method of watching a rewind of your day as if on video. See yourself get up out of bed, walk backwards to the bathroom, turn on the light, squeeze the toothpaste back into the tube … running through your night back into the afternoon. By this time, your mind will have found this so unusual a process that it will be glad to shut down.

When you need to survive after a poor night

- **Have catnaps.** Prominent people like Toscanini, Sir Winston Churchill and Margaret Thatcher at the peak of their careers only slept for four or five hours per night. They perfected the art of nodding off for a few minutes during travelling or waiting periods. Recent studies have shown that a ten-minute nap is actually more beneficial than a longer one. An afternoon rest recharges batteries, even if you don't actually sleep.

- **Curb worry.** Resist the temptation to worry about the number of hours you might have slept: 'Oh dear, it's 3am, that means I'll only have four hours' sleep. I'll be a wreck tomorrow.' Some people simply need less sleep than others, and as we grow older our bodies require even less. Worrying about insomnia is just a waste of time which could be used more usefully elsewhere.

- **Try an air ionizer.** This helps those who sleep poorly because nasal problems or headaches cause shallow breathing. If it is not dealt with, it can leave you sluggish the next morning.

Less successful sleep-aids

- **Use sleeping pills with caution.** Whereas medication may be useful to break a worrying cycle of insomnia, it should be used with careful medical supervision. The side effects of sleeping pills, such as a dry mouth, may be unnerving to the performer. They may leave us feeling groggy and they alter crucial dream processes. Herbal or homoeopathic versions involve fewer health risks.

Professor Peter Yellowlees of the University of Queensland's medical faculty comments:

I agree with avoiding 'sleeping pills', but readers should know about the different types. People should not use tranquillisers just to send themselves to sleep (particularly Benzodiazapines such as Valium and Mogadon, the two most widely used sleeping tablets).

These types of sleeping pills are addictive and are used far too much within the general population. They also lose their potency or effectiveness after a few days, so many people escalate the dose inappropriately. It is important to not make rapid alterations to medication regimes and only to do so in conjunction with the doctor who prescribed them. If medications are being used for illnesses such as depression or anxiety, it is best not to change these medications at all prior to any important performances.

- **Avoid alcohol. While a modest amount of alcohol may increase the time we sleep, research has shown that the level and quality of that sleep are less beneficial. Alcohol consumption reduces both the slow-wave deep sleep and the rapid eye movement sleep. Also, it depletes the body of some of the B vitamins which are important in the normal rhythms of the sleep-wake cycle and in brain activity. It causes loss of magnesium, a mineral which increases relaxation.**
- **Avoid caffeine. Some people are particularly affected by caffeine and even a cup of coffee in the late afternoon interferes with their night's sleep. Avoid it for seven hours before going to sleep.**

Caffeine is a central nervous system stimulant which causes higher blood pressure, increased heart rate, wakefulness, diuresis. It causes an increase in gastric secretion and is potentially addictive. It may exacerbate the symptoms of anxiety disorders and increase the need for sedative medicines. If moderate to heavy users try to withdraw, they may experience lethargy, irritability, hypersomnia and severe headache. Caffeine may exacerbate the symptoms of anxiety disorders and increase the need for sedative medicines. Limit intake and try decaffeinated beverages. Be aware that appreciable amounts of caffeine are also found in chocolate and in pharmaceutical stimulants, analgesics and flu and sinus medications.

Eat healthy food

Excess sugar depletes the immune system and can precipitate depression and anxiety attacks, whereas nutritious food strengthens the nervous system, helping us to cope with stress. It's better to rely on a backlog of nutritious meals rather than attempt to cram in nutrients at the last minute. Your body needs at least twelve to fourteen days before dietary improvements can be effective.

General food requirements

Eat wholesome, fresh salads, fruit and vegetables daily. Warm milk and carbohydrate such as a slice of bread cause endorphins to relax the body. These foods should be an integral part of the diet, rather than a quick fix before an event.

Food requirements prior to a performance

Why aren't performers, like athletes, given strict diets chosen by nutritionists according to our energy levels and the length of time it takes to digest food? For example, eggs and boiled milk pass out of the stomach in two hours, whereas sardines take nine!

Remember how sluggish we feel after a big meal? We'd much rather sleep than exert ourselves. Many well-meaning performers expect that a protein meal like steak will ensure high energy levels. In fact, the task of digesting animal fat draws oxygen from the body tissues, causing sleepiness. While consistent protein intake is important as part of a balanced diet, the secret is to maintain steady optimum blood-sugar levels. Complex carbohydrates (wholegrains, potatoes, bananas, legumes) supply these more efficiently.

Although nuts are a good source of energy, singers and reed players should avoid them before a concert because they might catch in the throat or on the reed. Milk, bananas and chocolate cause phlegm.

Rather than risk the drop in blood sugar after a large meal, causing a hypoglycemic attack, during pressured days consider five or six small meals. Stress slows down the digestive system and it is not advisable to eat a huge meal before a performance. On the other hand, one needs optimum energy, so eat a healthy snack about two hours before performing. This releases energy and endurance when needed, while allowing time for the food to leave the stomach to avoid that bloated, heavy feeling.

Sugar is a major pitfall for the unwary. When we need to boost energy, we automatically reach for sugar in some form – fizzy drinks, chocolate, sweets. Even many 'healthy' fruit juices contain a high sugar content.

Hitting the system with a big dose of sugar can shock the pancreas into making too much insulin, which dramatically lowers blood sugar. The body goes on emergency alert, sending an SOS signal to the adrenal glands, which send out adrenaline to find more sugar. A low sugar-response can confuse us by making us feel simultaneously edgy, worn, hungry and yet full. On the one hand, low blood sugar creates tiredness, sluggishness and fuzzy thinking. On the other hand, the adrenaline response to meet the low-sugar emergency stimulates the body, causing insomnia, irritation, restlessness, quickened heartbeat and apprehension.

If you are persistently conscious of excessive irritability, depression, anxiety, poor concentration and memory, confusion, headache, body twitches and tremors, cold hands and feet, consider the possibility of low blood sugar.

Some people are badly affected by monosodium glutamate used in Chinese restaurants (that stand-by of the busy performer on out-of-town gigs).

So what can I eat before a performance? A light meal of some carbohydrate, like bread with honey, or a bland rice dish, gives energy without weighing down the digestive system. Starchy foods allow slow release energy. Bananas and oatmeal biscuits contain fibre and are easily digested. Fish, a light protein, is known as an excellent brain food. Egg or pasta are light and easily digested. One performer eats several raw eggs before going on stage. He says, 'They go down easily and soothe my throat.' Try them in an eggnog.

If your stomach feels too uneasy to face any food, consider the value of drinking fruit juices, preferably freshly prepared and diluted with water. Avoid citrus juices: being acidic, they may set your delicate stomach even more on edge. Grape juice is a source of quick energy, relieves nervous exhaustion and also clears phlegm. Juices made from strawberry, cucumber, lettuce and parsley are all excellent tonics for helping to reduce nervous anxiety. Many singers and speakers swear by pineapple juice.

But don't throw them all into the juicer together! Mix compatible fruits or vegetables – carrot with parsley and lettuce; strawberry with apple; or apple, carrot and banana. However, most people prefer to avoid salad foods like lettuce and cucumber as they may cause repeating and indigestion.

Herbal teas made from catmint, thyme and valerian have been used for hundreds of years to calm the nervous system. Sage is known as a tonic for the brain and nerves, maté is good for exhaustion and tiredness and as a general tonic. Chamomile helps reduce nervousness and insomnia.

A good multi-vitamin supplement can improve overall ability to cope with demands. When under pressure, I have found magnesium orotate and Vitamin B6 helpful, though a balanced Vitamin B Complex is generally preferable. Zinc combats mental exhaustion, as does potassium or soya lecithin. Consult with a naturopath, chemist or dietitian for your own particular needs.

Some natural dietary sources are:

• Vitamin B: brewer's yeast, wheat germ, egg yolk, meat, fish, cabbage. (Some people may be allergic to brewer's yeast and prefer vitamin supplements.) Vitamin B6 is helpful in alleviating premenstrual tension; B12 and B3 decrease depression. Check with a naturopath or nutritionist for dosage.

• Magnesium: almonds, barley, figs, dates, walnuts, wholemeal, wheat, corn, beans, oats, peas, rye, spinach, rice, lentils, fish.

• Potassium: olives, bananas, beans, peas, lentils, raisins, dates, almonds, figs, potatoes, walnuts, apple.

What to drink before a performance

Singers and speakers avoid milk as it creates phlegm. Some find that beer does also, and any alcohol risks the muscle control, clear head and concentration needed on stage. ('I can't control my tongueing after champagne,' says one oboist.) Excess caffeine can give you the jitters.

Water is vital for optimum functioning. The body requires at least six to eight glasses of water daily for best functioning. This should be increased in times of pressure. Increased water intake helps performers as it improves concentration and mental and physical coordination, alleviates mental fatigue, lifts energy levels and allows relaxed communication.

Our bodies are made up of about seventy per cent water, which is an excellent conductor of electrical energy. The electrical and chemical actions of the central nervous system and brain depend on efficient conduction of electrical currents to pass messages between the brain and sensory organs. Water intake must be increased during periods of stress as psychological and environmental stress dehydrate the body.

My husband and I took an orchestra on a three-week tour across Australia, travelling long days with up to twelve-hour stretches by bus. There was no water cooler in the bus and often on arrival we would rush straight into rehearsals or performances, with no time for a drink. Many avoided the taste of strange waters in 'foreign' cities. Looking back, I realised that most of us became exhausted and less resilient as the tour went on due to basic dehydration. In planning subsequent tours, we have checked that buses have water fountains or else have stipulated that everyone brings a water bottle.

Warm drinks are more soothing than cold ones: heat relaxes, cold constricts. Iced water is less easily absorbed by the body than water at room temperature. Deepak Chopra recommends frequent sips of hot water. Filtered or natural mineral spring waters are generally popular, especially when touring, as tummy upsets can result from strange chemicals and unsavoury greeblies.

However, there is a problem. Most performers notice that nerves induce frequency of urination. This is because the smooth muscle of the genito-urinary system contracts when the sympathetic system is activated as part of the adrenaline rush. Cardiac racing can also cause diaresis.

Coping with frequent urination and diarrhoea

What performer has not experienced the need to frequent the bathroom before going on stage? Film star Dustin Hoffman, performing *The Merchant of Venice* in London, found live acting far more stressful than filming:

The man (the audience) had all come to see as Shylock is
nervously sitting on the loo. He has been in the lavatory so often
and so long in the days before the opening that the cast have put a
plaque up on the door, reading 'Dustin Hoffman is Here', which
we have all signed.

(*Dustin Hoffman*, Ronald Bergan, p.1)

Drink plenty of water earlier in the day, then limit the fluid intake in the hour before performing to avoid the need to go to the bathroom. If necessary, relieve mouth dryness with rinses or gargling.

For diarrhoea, buy Gastrolite from a chemist, or a doctor can prescribe the drug Immodium. The onset is two and a half hours if taken in tablet form. As with all drugs, there is a potential for adverse reactions which could compromise the performance. Common adverse reactions of antidiarrheals include dry mouth, drowsiness and fatigue. However, not everyone experiences these reactions.

Naturopathic cures are Doctor Bach's Rescue Remedy, gelsemium or homeopathic Ipecac. (Note that the medical form of Ipecac induces vomiting.) An old wives' remedy of a few little nips of brandy is one of the few reasons for recommending alcohol as a curative before concerts! I can vouch for its effectiveness from personal experience:

While on a busy country examining schedule, I suffered a bad
gastric attack. I telephoned the teacher in charge to warn her that
cancellation seemed the only safe course.

'No worries!' she responded blithely. 'I know an old English
country remedy that works a treat.' Ten minutes later, she arrived
at my motel. She produced a bottle of brandy, a small glass and
several packets of peppermints. 'Because your reputation would
be ruined if candidates smelled brandy on the examiner's breath!
Now, down the hatch.'

'I can't drink now, especially on an empty stomach,' I protested.

'All the better. It burns as it goes down. Just a sip every hour or so
and you'll be better.'

I wanted to crawl away home, but what was there to lose? By mid-
morning the diarrhoea had vanished.

Dealing with dry mouth and saliva problems

Nerves present in different ways to different people: some feel discomfort because of a dry mouth, others from excess saliva. First, dry mouth. Check if any medications you take may worsen the problem. A pharmacist can supply an over-the-counter liquid spray solution that creates artificial saliva.

Before going on stage, drink a little warm water, then suffice with rinsing. Warm water relaxes the vocal cords, but cold tightens. A cup of sweetened tea with milk will bring back the saliva. Unfortunately, such inconveniences usually arise on stage when we cannot rush off to boil the kettle, but that thermos backstage is a comforting anticipation. Suck a boiled lolly, cough lozenge or slice of lemon. Bring along a small bottle of vinegar; its smell prompts saliva. Chew sugarless gum before performing.

A singer sat onstage through Beethoven's lengthy *Ninth Symphony*. By the time her solo was due, she was dry-mouthed. She solved the problem by biting hard on her tongue. Other solutions are to press the tip of the tongue on the hard palette near the teeth ridge. Subtle sucking movements and yawning promote saliva.

Michael McCallion explores remedies beyond glasses of water:

Work on the [Alexander Technique] head/neck/back relationship may tackle this at its root and will certainly help to get stage fright under control. Lemon is particularly helpful if you're working in a dry atmosphere ... Theatres, film and television studios and recording booths nearly always have dry overheated atmospheres; this can cause dry mouth even without the anxiety.

(*The Voice Book*, Michael McCallion, p. 219)

Second, excess saliva. When the sympathetic nervous system is activated by the fight/flight response, one factor is that the salivary glands secrete more thick, viscid saliva compounds. If you often experience excess saliva, prime yourself backstage with a thermos of black tea to dry up your mouth.

Even experienced speakers and singers may choke momentarily on excessive saliva, with resulting strain to their voice. Either you must miss a few words or notes to swallow, or else there is no option but to spray it out.

Maintain overall health with 'natural' remedies

Many people – myself included – find that massage, acupuncture or an adjustment from a chiropractor help their general state of health and their ability to cope. If you have neck soreness or headaches coming from the back of the head, check with a chiropractor if your spine needs adjustment.

Homeopaths give drops which alleviate nervous stress – for example, gelsemium or the Dr Bach Rescue Remedy, which aids centring, focusing and alleviates panic, exhaustion, tiredness and fear. Rock Rose is particularly helpful for nerves. Homeopathic diluted aconite alleviates feelings of fear, fright and anxiety. Another 'flower remedy', olive, relieves exhaustion and lifts energy levels.

Clarinettist Micaela Nathan can vouch for Rescue Remedy:

I performed a concert at a big cultural festival before my students, the whole school music department, my colleagues. I really felt I had to prove myself as a musician and as a teacher. Stupid me! I picked the hardest piece, one which I had only played once before, several years ago, so I was very nervous.

I totally relied on my mental preparation, centred my energies and was really helped by taking Rescue Remedy drops four drops every five minutes before going on stage. (There are no harmful effects from taking it often; in fact, the more frequently I take it the better it works.) Once I began to play, it all clicked into place and I sailed through the piece.

Acupuncture has been used by the Chinese for four thousand years to treat a wide range of medical complaints, including tension and headaches. Treatment from a qualified practitioner can help enormously. It is illegal for unqualified people to attempt such treatment.

However, we can treat ourselves with acupressure with considerable success. Press with the tip of the index finger or thumb on contact points or sore spots with a firm, but not painful pressure. Press a few seconds, release, then repeat as often as feels comfortable. It isn't possible to over-treat: the longer and the more often, the better.

Some people prevent nausea and travel sickness by taking remedies which include that useful plant, ginger, or by wearing acupuncture magnets worn on elastic wristbands. This is also applicable to stomach nerves in performance. Relief can be felt by massaging or pressing on the pressure point (called Neigun or PC6) which is located about two finger breadths above the wrist crease, between the two main tendons on the inner forearm. Press firmly or stroke towards the wrist. (Stroking from this point towards the elbow can induce vomiting.) This pressure point is also useful for treating shortness of breath, insomnia and anxiety. Massage or press tender points in a radius of five centimetres around the navel to relieve emotional stress.

Lemon and ginger tea bags are available – even better, infuse fresh chopped ginger in hot water. A colleague swears by the following old wives' remedy for motion sickness and nerves. His wife suffered so badly from travel sickness that an air steward was heard to exclaim: 'I can't believe it!' She tried rubbing a cooling liniment such as Vicks in her navel, covered with sticking plaster and thereafter travelled without any nausea.

The need to exercise care with drugs and alcohol

Beta blockers are drugs which may be prescribed by a doctor or psychiatrist to block the adrenaline reaction and anxiety symptoms. They slow the heart rate, reduce sweating and tremors, alleviate a dry mouth or the jitters – that is, they do not stop nerves, but lessen their symptoms. Beta blockers are not addictive, although their use may become a habit if the sufferer comes to rely on them. They should only be taken on medical advice, adhering to the exact prescription. If abused, they can be dangerous for people prone to diabetes, certain heart conditions, bronchitis, depression, hay fever and asthma. There is some indication they may trigger asthma. Some people have noted side effects, including: dizziness, lightheadedness, nightmares, hallucinations, lethargy, insomnia, visual disturbances, diarrhoea, drowsiness, loss of appetite, cold hands and feet, and loss of hair. Some who have taken beta blockers before a test have had difficulty with memory and expressing information.

Try out their suitability well before a performance. It would be shattering to discover a previously unsuspected cardiac or asthma condition while onstage. Beta blockers are often ineffective in cases where anxiety is associated with depression; counselling or anti-depressants might more successfully tackle the depression. In fact, beta blockers may exacerbate the depression. Professor Peter Yellowlees of the University of Queensland explains:

Beta blockers reduce the physiological manifestations of anxiety, but not the psychological causes of this. As such, they can easily become an 'emotional crutch' which may be hard for the performer to leave behind. It is clearly best to try non-drug means first. If people do start using beta blockers, then they really should be combined with a cognitive behavioural treatment program designed to allow them to learn physiological control over their bodies and therefore not need the drugs in any case.

Having said this, there are a very few people who do find it impossible in the short run to control their physiological symptoms of anxiety, and who are therefore given a 'kick start' by beta blockers, while hoping to stop using them as soon as possible.

Pianist Carson Dron's experience with beta blockers backs this advice:

I had a terrible problem with the shakes while at university, so a doctor recommended that I try beta blockers. They did stop the shaking and gave me confidence to face performance again. They took me over my barrier and, after three or four months, I thought, 'I don't need to worry about my nerves – I don't need the beta blockers any more.' So I stopped taking them.

But I do know a lot of performers who rely on them and I would advise people to be very careful. I did find it more unpleasant playing when taking beta blockers, as they made me feel cold, detached from the audience. My mind wandered and I had concentration lapses. But, yes, it was a positive experience in that I overcame my fear of shaking.

Violist and composer Brett Dean says:

I hear of students who take beta blockers before relatively minor stresses such as a music lesson. Our society tends to offer a pill for every problem. Thus, they tell the problem to be quiet rather than find a solution.

At one stage, I let the nerves grow too much, but what I learned will stand me in good stead. Now, I might still shake, but that doesn't matter. If I stop being nervous before a performance, then it is time to stop playing.

Swedish flautist Jan Westerlund makes a valid point:

When I used beta blockers, I played quite well technically, but my feelings were lost. Why should we play music without feelings?

Violinist/conductor Antoni Bonetti says:

At one stage I tried beta blockers. Physically, they improved my muscular control of the violin bow, though I also experienced cold sweats. I didn't feel particularly confident as my anxious thoughts were still with me. Eventually, I realised that on some of these occasions I had flu symptoms, which weakened my strength of mind. This caused me to dwell on negative past concert issues. The sickness exacerbated insecurities. I found that by maintaining good health, I was able to deal with the issues without the use of beta blockers.

Many performing artists have found at some time that they need a stiff drink in order to face their audience. The euphorients of alcohol, tranquillisers and drugs depress the nervous system and are addictive. They diminish one's control of the situation and are rarely a successful means of coping with problems. They may appear to help, in that one is less aware, and in such a desensitised state may imagine things to be better than they are – hardly a satisfactory coping mechanism. Remember, too, that excessive drinking destroys brain cells.

We must realise that alcohol is a depressant drug. The first one or two drinks that people take essentially tend to depress their inhibitions, which makes them feel somehow braver, more socially successful and sometimes more confident with the encouragement of this 'Dutch courage'. The evidence is very clear, however, that even this first one or two drinks have a depressant effect on physical performance and, whilst people may feel they are going to perform better with a 'drink under their belt', this is unlikely.

The creative personality is particularly prone to alcohol abuse. At first, it may seem a way to maintain the highs, but performing artists are especially prone to mood swings, from elation to despair and back again. Unfortunately, where at first they might think they play better after a glass or two ... or three ... usually they lose judgment. It is all too easy to come to rely on that lift, especially as sociable performing artists naturally gravitate to the bar before or after a show.

Actor Anthony Hopkins realised these dangers: 'For many artists, actors and musicians, alcohol becomes their rocket-fuel. And it eventually can burn them up. It didn't get me because I suppose I suddenly became frightened of where I was going – down to Hell in a wheelbarrow'.

Conductor and pianist Tommy Tycho has always insisted on working with sober musicians: 'In past decades, some players rolled into work drunk, but it happens rarely nowadays. The competition for work is so fierce that you just can't take the risk of dismissal. You really have to look behind you because dozens of good musicians are vying for your chair.'

The need to unwind after a performance makes drinking all the more natural. (Avoid phoning actors, dancers and singers in the early morning after a performance, for they were probably out eating, drinking and winding down until late. Vocalist Feodor Chaliapin refused the offer of a well-paid 11am engagement: 'Madame, at that hour, I cannot even spit!')

It's wise to drink a few healthy glasses of water or juice before progressing to a stronger tipple. Often we drink more alcohol than we need because we don't realise that genuine thirst needs quenching.

How often in the past have we put ourselves under increased pressure, oblivious of the ill-effects of existing on excess junk-food, caffeine and alcohol? Or blamed ourselves for a poor performance when we had turned a deaf ear to our body's pleas for more sleep? Imagine how much better we can cope with the demands of performance by adopting some simple, basic lifestyle changes to improve our general health.

As society has become resistant to the benefits of antibiotics the simplistic concept of taking a pill to cure every ill is less valid. It becomes increasingly obvious that we must take more responsibility for our well-being by preventive methods. A healthy and balanced lifestyle and diet, adequate sleep and relaxation are one facet. There are other aspects of our daily routines which hinder us from performing to our best ability. We need to consider our whole entity;

let us examine more physical, mental and spiritual aspects, so we may release even more blocked energy. Chapter 8 shows us how we can positively improve our ability to cope and thus to communicate.

Summary

- **Adequate sleep and nutritious food are important to ensure confident performance. A light meal of carbohydrate (bread, rice, pasta) about two hours before a performance gives optimum energy without a heavy stomach.**
- **Fruit juices give energy. Sufficient water is necessary for overall functioning.**
- **There are ways of managing frequent urination, diarrhoea, dry mouth and excess saliva.**
- **Natural cures have good effects and less likelihood of side effects or addiction than drugs or alcohol.**

8

How to prepare by revitalising the whole person

*Just as other pianists, I have given ... good, medium and
bad concerts. Three-quarters of my life is lived in
conditions entirely wrong for concert work. I always found
it especially easy to play after a holiday; there were no
small mishaps, no feeling of weariness from which I
sometimes suffer ... where I am snowed under by my
teaching work.*

Pianist Heinrich Neuhaus

A TIRED PERSON IS MORE PREY to fears and nerves. How can we
recharge our energies, revitalise the whole person, body, mind and
spirit? Many avenues may be explored with excellent results.

Exercise and recreation

Recreation means, in fact, to re-create. Through this and its partner,
physical exercise, we are renewed. There is no real work without real
rest. We need exercise and recreation to balance and revitalise our
lives and to counter staleness. Intersperse practice times with some
breathing spaces, stretching exercises, a walk or a run. Look at the
horizon to keep your perspective and freshen your vision.

All performers need those strong, resilient bodies of athletes and
dancers. The body contains groups of small muscles and large
muscles. When muscles are weakened through minimal use, the blood
flows less efficiently, carrying less oxygen to the relevant organs and
brain.

Choose activities that you actually enjoy, rather than merely
endure, or enthusiasm may wane. Whether through aerobics, golf, a

trampoline, gymnasium or your own walking and exercise program at home, regular, relaxing movement keeps the body toned. Swimming is especially relaxing as the water supports the body's weight. A regular swimming program in the months before a big performance is as important to me as the physical practice on my instrument. It increases my vital lung power, lessens tension levels and improves my ability to cope.

Breathing

The old cure for nerves of 'ten deep breaths' is still valid. It is also apt that the word 'inspiration' relates to breathing, our very life-force. All musicians, not just singers, wind and brass players, benefit from focus on deep breathing. It is crucial for voice projection.

When we are under pressure, we all instinctively tend to hold our breath – a survival mechanism learned as children – and this tenses our bodies. Consequently, many performers find themselves trapped in ramrod, frozen postures. It causes insufficient oxygen flow to the brain and thus a lower energy level. It even causes an imbalance between the left and right sides of the body and brain.

We need to retrain such a response, to change the pattern when the emergency is over. A few moments of slow, deep breathing with a hand on your forehead releases such stress; the action brings energy away from the hypothalamus, which is the fight/ flight centre of the brain, towards the neo-cortex, the centre of logic and rational thought.

Just as a car engine cannot be driven without fuel, so a singer, speaker or wind player cannot produce full tone without plenty of air. That means allowing for more than enough air, refilling the lungs before running out. We usually refill the petrol tank before we putter to a stop by the side of a busy motorway!

Breathing is a natural, normal action, one which has kept us alive all our lives without conscious thought. Watch a baby or pet sleeping. See the movement as their diaphragm and ribs rise and fall as they breathe. That's how easy it should be.

Exhalation

To discover the energy and strength of a full, deep breath, first exhale. Empty your lungs with a gusty, audible sigh. Release all that stale air. Carbon dioxide, that waste part of our air, is heavier than oxygen, so it sinks to the bottom of our lungs. Empty it out, give an extra huff and wait a few seconds until you really need another breath. When it comes, naturally, instinctively, it will be deep and satisfying … and correct. Of course, musicians are at the mercy of the rhythmic pulse so many inhalations will be quick, but they can use occasional rest bars to expel excess air.

Inhalation

Luciano Pavarotti told how he was not complete master of his voice until he learned correct diaphragmatic breathing from Dame Joan Sutherland. He watched, listened and placed his hands on her ribs to feel their expansion as she inhaled.

The lungs and diaphragm are often mentioned in a singing teacher's first sentence. We all know where the lungs are, but where is this diaphragm? Many natural activities show how we constantly use the diaphragm in everyday living. To locate it, place a hand just above your navel and try these examples:

- **Go out into the garden and smell a flower. Notice how the breath came naturally from just above the navel?**
- **Fake a cough, yawn or sneeze. Did you feel movement above your tummy?**
- **Take a breath thinking 'eee', then another on an 'ohhh' as in 'hot'. Notice that the former felt shallow, tight, unsatisfying while the 'ohhh' breath was quick, deep, easy, and lasted longer?**
- **Hold a piece of paper against the wall for a few seconds by blowing a steady stream of air at it.**
- **Light a candle. Blow steadily so that the flame tilts, then blow it out. Did you feel the tightening of the solar plexus?**

These actions are natural, involuntary and use correct diaphragm breathing.

The diaphragm is a sheet of muscle which separates the chest area, containing the lungs, from the abdomen. As we breathe in, the diaphragm, together with your lower ribs, expands downwards and outwards, causing the chest to expand. When you exhale, the diaphragm involuntarily returns to its position, pushing the air on its way. The tummy muscles can reinforce the air column in a smooth stream, which is what teachers mean by reminders to 'support'.

So what is 'support'? Michael McCallion describes it:

Support for the voice is strength with direction and it comes about when the breathing muscles are working in a state of coordination with a good head/neck/back relationship. To put it simply, it is the refusal to collapse and the physical means whereby you make your breath last as long as you want, at the pressure you need to make whatever sound you want, at whatever volume, pitch and resonance is called for.

The important thing to note here is what is happening to the spine because, if the spine is maintaining its lengthening tendency, the rib cage cannot collapse downwards. However, the ribs are left free to move. During the out-breath ... the chest is not seen to slump in the slightest; the shoulders are completely uninvolved and stay open and still.

(*The Voice Book*, Michael McCallion, p. 37)

Place a hand over the lower ribs at the side or ask a friend to do so. Gently push out the air. Feel the ribs and lower back muscles expand as you inhale – for your lungs expand right around to your back. Or make a diamond shape by joining both index fingers and long fingers placed just above your navel. As you breathe in, the fingers should separate, then meet as you exhale.

Just as singers, actors and speakers are their 'instrument', so, too, wind and brass players are a continuation of their instruments. My clarinet 'extends' through my mouth, into a wide, opened pipeline right down through the neck and chest, to the complex of diaphragm muscles which activate the process. Seeing this perspective lessens the likelihood of tension of the throat and muscles which surround the vocal cords. This constriction causes sharpened pitch. If I concentrate on pushing the column of air out in a smooth flow, I am less likely to tense other muscles. Tonal production and ease of tongue action are improved.

It is not only singers, speakers and wind players who benefit. Many string players, including violinist Yehudi Menuhin, have found deep breathing a rich wellspring from which natural phrasing flows.

Notice your breathing patterns away from the instrument, perhaps while lying relaxed on the beach or drowsing in bed before sleeping. Lie comfortably, with the knees bent, a hand above the navel. Slowly breathe out … right out. Empty your lungs … Give an extra huff (imagine the tide drawing right out to sea). Wait until you really need that breath, then breathe in deeply.

Having emptied the lungs first, you will breathe deeply, correctly, without any conscious thought. The lower chest area will lift, then the upper chest. As you breathe out, notice that your lower chest subsides, then the upper chest. Still lying down, relaxed, place two books, one on the diaphragm, the other on the chest. If you are breathing correctly, the lower book will lift first while both inhaling and exhaling.

Vocalists, wind and brass players often have to snatch quick breaths and may transfer this habit to everyday life. It is important to inhale slowly where possible, both in warm-ups and when the score or text allows.

Some teachers suggest exercises for building up breath capacity. Many recommend students 'develop' their breathing apparatus by lying down and lifting the telephone directory with the diaphragm. My preference is to make sure that we understand correct breathing and make a habit of it. Regular exercise, such as swimming, aerobics or walking is a much more pleasant way to develop capacity.

Or lie relaxed and count slowly as you exhale right out, wait, then inhale and hold. You will find that your capacity and consequent counting increases over a period of time.

It is possible to create tension through trying too hard with breathing. Remember that inhalation is a very natural process.

Breathing in everyday living

Many singers and wind players become accustomed to breathing through the mouth, as this enables them to inhale more air. In fact, nostril breathing is healthier for everyday living. A pitfall is to transfer the snatching of quick breaths demanded by music into everyday living.

In normal healthy living, we should breathe comfortably, each breath taking perhaps three seconds rather than one. Slow inhalations are more soothing, whereas constant quick gasps may induce a feeling of unease. Studies of prisoners of war have shown that people who have an instinctively slower pattern of breathing, lengthening the pause between exhalation and inhalation, are more healthy and cope better with stress.

Waste rather than hoard your air!

Many remember to inhale a full breath, but fail to understand the importance of following through with the diaphragm support while exhaling, exerting slight pressure with the abdominal muscles. Thus, some wind players 'tickle' their instruments, not filling the pipe with sufficient air; they unnecessarily hoard their air, afraid that they won't have enough. Air is still free! Politicians have not managed to impose a tax on it. We can use as much as we need, waste it even, without concern or guilt. In fact, all the better if we do use it lavishly, for when we empty our lungs as completely as possible, we then follow with a deeper inspiration. If we hoard our air, we may panic that we don't have enough, but by thoroughly exhaling we can take in as much as we need. Those who hoard their breath run short, but those who give it away freely have plenty, for they create the space for more.

On the other hand, we often need to gauge how fast air should be expelled. With particularly long phrases, it is sensible to not let too much air out in the first few seconds. Some shorter phrases may require only a small or medium intake.

Breath nourishes the fingers

Don't we all sometimes unconsciously hold our breath when a passage bristling with semiquavers and double sharps approaches? During such a panic attack, our systems shut down, but our heart rate and respiration increase, creating muscle tension. In this way, playing of technically difficult passages is often further inhibited by breath-restriction. My own music, and that of most of my students, invariably sports a long pencilled arrow under difficult passages – my shorthand for 'Blow! Support!' Focusing on breathing helps to free you from worrying about fingers.

In fact, insufficient oxygen flow due to breath holding may slow finger fluency. When challenged into an adrenaline rush by the stress of the difficult passage, the sympathetic nervous system works overtime channelling blood to the central organs – and away from the extremities.

To overcome technical passages, relax and focus on slow breathing. Preparation can include yoga-type exercises. Yogi have discovered that expanding the waistline through deep breathing relaxes the body and mind. They use deep breathing as a path to meditation, relaxation and general health.

Plan ahead for good breathing

Experienced players anticipate restricted breathing when under pressure. Play, sing or speak through the material well before the event, pencilling in normal breathing places. Bracket extra emergency breathing points at appropriate places. This means you will not disturb the (breath) flow by breathing in (huff) mid-phrase, which quite spoils the (gasp) effect, doesn't it?

When under pressure, it is comforting to see a suitable breathing place coming up. Much of the pressure of 'not having enough air' is caused by fear of running out. Pencil in breath marks at occasional rest bars where you will have time to breathe out before inhaling.

This will reduce the likelihood of hyperventilating due to desperately snatched shallow breaths. Many performers recognise that pent-up feeling of not having enough air when actually you are clogged up with too much air which you are not able to exhale.

Remember to inhale early enough so phrase openings are poised, and relate breath speed to the tempo of the music; a slow breath in a Largo movement, a quick inhalation for Presto.

Shallow breathing

A sure sign of shallow breathing is when your shoulders lift as you inhale and, instead of the waist expanding, it hunches in. Try it. Do you feel a choked, gasping sensation? It is the opposite reaction to deep breathing.

Having heard me teaching students to breathe, my three sons asked me to check if their own breathing was correct. Perhaps because they tried too hard, each in turn demonstrated exactly how *not* to breathe.

When we are relaxed, breathing is a natural, easy process. Relax, exhale completely and let your instinctive reactions do the rest.

Posture

Breathing is closely linked with good posture. A defensive, hunched posture restricts our lungs, limits capacity.

What is 'correct' posture? The very word makes people instinctively over-compensate, often causing more problems. Find a natural, comfortable balance this way: Stand up against a wall, with head and feet about ten centimetres away from the wall. Lightly press the torso, from shoulders to buttocks, against the wall as much as possible, given the inherent S-bend of the spine. Bend your knees slightly, thus unlocking their tension and tilting your pelvis forward a little. Do you notice how your chest has expanded out into that barrel shape common to good singers?

If accustomed to poor posture, this may seem forced and unnatural. Stand up against the wall for a few moments through the day to become accustomed to it. Make it a habit. Sing, speak or play a sound in this posture, and you will probably be surprised at the improved projection, depth and quality of your tone.

The Alexander Technique

Habitual poor posture and repeated body misuse can damage the voice, as Australian actor Frederick Matthias Alexander discovered early last century. His recurrent loss of voice during performances threatened his career as an actor.

Alexander spent desperate hours in front of a mirror, observing the muscles used in speech. He noted breathing interference and some curious movements of his head and neck, not only when he spoke, but also when he merely thought of performing. The most common one, a tightening of the head backwards and downwards into the chest, was eventually proved to be a major cause of many common illnesses. When he learned to use his body correctly, his voice problems ceased.

His Alexander Technique evolved into a system of therapy which focuses awareness on body usage, balance and posture, based on the premise that use affects functioning. It is a relaxed system of non-doing and awareness rather than busy exercises. A major focus is on restoring the natural habit of stretching and uplifting our spine, freeing and opening out our bodies. Mental directions to the crucial muscles and body parts achieve a sense of 'up-ness' to counteract gravity's compression. By eliminating rigid fixing habits, the back widens and spine lengthens, the neck 'lets go' of tension.

An easy but important exercise is simply to lie on your back on the floor. Support your head with a couple of books, just enough to be comfortable. Bend your knees, feet flat on the floor, slightly apart. Let your neck relax. Allow your spine to lengthen, your back flattening against the floor. If you lie in this position for about twenty minutes a day, you will find you feel more awake, energised and aware of your body posture.

The Alexander Technique has proved so effective that many music and drama institutions make such classes compulsory. How does this help nervous performers?

Let us go back to our basic fight-or-flight mechanism. When threatened by that sabre-toothed tiger in our cave or that rival sitting smugly in the audience front row, an instinctive reaction is to hunch up the shoulders protectively, constricting and shortening the spine. We pull the back of the neck closed, as if fearing a blow to the neck. This panic reaction also inhibits the crucial breath flow. McCallion writes:

> One of the two major nerves responsible for our breathing takes as its point of origin the third, fourth and fifth cervical vertebrae. If we badly upset the relationship between these vertebrae, the uninterrupted and continuing exchange of in-breath for out-breath, the rhythmicity of our breathing cycle, is adversely affected. The other major nerve activates our breathing starts working in overdrive, and we feel short of breath no matter how much breath we actually have!

(*The Voice Book*, Michael McCallion, p. 31)

Another Alexander action is the 'whispered aah', which improves freedom of the crucial neck hinge, opens the important bronchial throat passage and encourages deep, natural breathing. To do this, stand balanced and upright with the neck free. Smile broadly showing the teeth, which are lightly touching but unclenched. The jaw swings open easily while exhaling on a 'whispered aah'. Repeat.

This is the purest uninterrupted sound you can make. It is helpful for the stutterer or stammerer and even helps seasickness, hangovers and nausea. This is because it prevents the tension caused by shallow breathing and helps to change the stale air at the bottom of the lungs. It allows more oxygen into the bloodstream; you may well want to yawn or laugh as you release tension with the 'whispered aah'.

Relax the jaw ... with a good yawn

Singing and speech projection require a loose jaw and this also helps to prevent over-straining of the larynx. As fifty per cent of brain signals pass into the body through a junction box at the jaw, all areas will function more efficiently if locked jaws are freed.

Do you have a 'clicky' jaw or do you chew on one side only? Do you clench your teeth at night through tension? These may be due to dental or chiropractic problems affecting your temporomandibular (jaw) joint. A dentist can align your teeth and make a night plate. A chiropractic adjustment may improve this and many other related problems at the same time.

A big yawn is wonderfully relaxing. Let your jaw drop, your mouth sagging open. Massage the hinge of the jaw, just in front of the ear and under your cheek bones. Soon you will feel an irresistible urge to yawn deeply. Let it happen. This is one of nature's best remedies for tiredness and tension, as it releases toxins and waste material in the blood. It causes a strong downward movement of the diaphragm, pulls in more fresh air and releases the stiffness in the trunk muscles caused by tiredness. It improves circulation to the head and relaxes throat, jaw and face muscles. Consequently, vocal or musical tone and projection are radically improved.

Brain Gym and Applied Kinesiology

I often tell my students to switch off their try-hard button. While as performers we constantly strive to do our best, being over-zealous is self-defeating. The essence of trying involves doubt. The analytical left brain is not only a critic, but also a doubter. Focus your awareness on one single aspect of your playing. As passive observation is a right brain activity, that allows you to escape the critical and doubting words of the left try brain. Substitute negative self-talk admonishings to 'try' or 'make an effort' with positives like 'experiment' or 'challenge'.

These concepts are central to Educational Kinesiology, pioneered by educator and author Paul E. Dennison and his wife Gail. Their program, 'Brain Gym', was originally conceived to correct learning disabilities. In it, simple movements and Laterality Repatterning enable people to access those parts of the brain previously inaccessible to them. An action as natural and simple as walking is a form of 'cross-crawl', which in crossing the centre-line, enables whole-brain learning and expression. In the 'old days', when students marched into class, the young people's brains were primed and ready to receive their information.

Paul Dennison writes:

Why do some learners do so well while others do not? In Edu-K, we see that some individuals try too hard and 'switch-off' the brain-integration mechanisms necessary for complete learning. Information is received by the back brain as an 'impress', but is inaccessible to the front brain as an 'express'. This inability to express what is learned locks the student into a failure syndrome ...

Centring is the ability to cross the midline between the upper and lower body and the corresponding upper and lower brain functions ... The inability to stay centred results in irrational fear, fight-or-flight responses, or an inability to feel or express emotions.

(*Brain Gym: Teacher's Edition*, Paul E. Dennison & Gail E. Dennison, p. 2)

I observed how such exercises can 'switch on' the brain by having my clarinet students do some basic Brain Gym exercises. One, Karen, was particularly uncoordinated. She stumbled through numerous mistakes with little apparent idea of the music. After a few minutes of cross-crawl exercises, Karen played with such accuracy and ease that she sailed through the whole page.

I pursued Brain Gym first-hand with some lessons from a musician, Deborah Knott, who had successfully incorporated her Brain Gym studies into music teaching. 'Bring along your instrument and a musical problem that you'd like to improve,' she said before the first lesson. Recently, I had sight-read one of those movements that bristle with mean hemi-demi-semiquaver passages. I had been conscious of my brain shutting down, unable to sequence the relationships of the rhythms. I played the passage to Deborah with similar lack of coherence. We set an appropriate goal: 'To easily and fluently play this piece while sequencing the rhythm into patterns.'

After going through the four steps of the PACE system (outlined below) I played the same piece easily and fluently and sequenced the rhythm clearly. One bar hesitated, but I knew exactly how it should have been played and repeated it correctly. Even better, we both noticed that the tone sang more warm and clear and the phrases were musically shaped.

Brain Gym exercises can improve the learning stages of preparation. Any aspect can be tackled by applying a step-wise 'balance' procedure. Various exercises improve facility of a wide range of everyday experiences relating to effective functioning of both sides of the brain. (Many are directly related to performance projection.)

Soon after, I used the PACE warm-up before a quartet 'gig' performance and the first two hours flowed easily and enjoyably. Whereas normally I preferred to play only rehearsed works, on this occasion I happily sight-read new works with ease. By the middle of the night, I started to make some blunders. I noticed that I felt thirsty – significant, as the first vital step in the PACE sequence is to drink water.

A good drink and a few minutes of exercises during the break meant that the rest of the night proceeded smoothly and enjoyably. Since then, I have found that PACE has helped my poise and concentration both in practice, performance and general focus.

Remember our fight or flight response, associated with adrenaline rush? The body springs into survival mode, focusing electrical energy away from the neocortex towards the sympathetic nervous system. Adrenaline levels rise and electrical potential across the nerve membrane occurs as the body prepares for fight or flight.

The Brain Gym 'Energy Exercises and Postures for Deepening Attitudes' (found in the Dennisons' *Brain Gym: Teacher's Edition*) activate the neocortex, refocusing electrical energy back to the reasoning centres. This stimulates parasympathetic function and decreases the release of adrenaline. By increasing the electrical threshold across the nerve membrane, thought and action are again coordinated. The semicircular canals of the inner ear are stimulated by electrical activity which, in turn, activates the brainstem's reticular formation, which screens distracting from relevant information. It creates wakefulness, facilitating focus and attention in the rational centres of the brain. This improves concentration.

Four basic steps are known as PACE (Positive, Active, Clear, Energetic). The first step is simply to drink water. As a marathon runner Dr Dennison learned the many benefits of water. Water is an excellent conductor of electricity: 'All of the electrical and chemical actions of the brain and central nervous system are dependent on the conductivity of electrical currents between the brain and the sensory organs, facilitated by water.' (Dennison, p.24)

The second step is known as 'brain buttons'. Massage the soft tissue under the clavicle to the right and left sides of the sternum, while holding the navel with the other hand. Among other benefits, this activates the brain to send messages from the right brain hemisphere to the left side of the body and vice versa, increases blood supply to the brain and increases the flow of electromagnetic energy.

The third step is 'cross-crawl'. Alternately move one arm and its opposite leg and the other arm and its opposite leg. This accesses both brain hemispheres simultaneously and is an ideal warm-up to improve coordination, breathing and stamina, and to enhance hearing and vision.

The fourth step is known as 'hook-ups'. These postures connect the electrical circuits in the body. The mind and body relax as energy circulates through areas blocked through tension. The figure of eight pattern of connected arms and legs follows the energy flow lines of the body. The touching of fingertips balances and connects the two brain hemispheres. They are invaluable for emotional centring, for balance and coordination, deeper respiration, and for releasing emotional stress, especially before meeting a challenge such as performance.

It is also worthwhile to work on what are known as 'positive points' – emotional stress-release points. Touch or massage lightly above each eye, halfway between the hairline and the eyebrows. These points are the neurovascular balance points for the stomach meridian. People tend to hold stress in the abdomen, which causes nervous stomachs. The positive points bring blood flow from the hypothalamus to the frontal lobes, where rational thought occurs. This prevents the fight/flight response, so that a new response to the situation can be learned. Massaging these points also releases memory blocks ('I know this; it's on the tip of my tongue').

In the same way that electrical circuits in a house can become overloaded, neurological and physiological signals can become jammed and switch off, blocking the normal flow of brain-body communication. Both Western and Eastern medical authorities recognise the need to keep the electromagnetic circuits of the body (described as 'meridians' in the Chinese system of acupuncture) flowing freely.

At one stage, I started to feel 'stuck' – that my brain had jammed up, struggling to cope with a combination of unresolved past issues and new challenges. Sessions with my chiropractor, who practises Applied Kinesiology and Neuro Emotional Technique, were very helpful; using muscle testing, he could 'click' through various factors with the speed of a computer. We discovered where areas of nerve interference were occurring, how they created disorganisation within my nervous system (that is, they 'switched' me off) and how to correct them. Subsequently, this technique has been used to free various tensions, many held in the body for years as the result of a negative comment or incident.

Chiropractic and nutritional adjustment, avoiding certain

chemicals and preservatives, and resolving various mental and emotional issues also freed me from such blockages.

Applied Kinesiology employs a holistic approach which deals with the physical, chemical, emotional and spiritual aspects of one's health. It discovers areas of nerve interference and offers solutions and appropriate treatment.

Applied Kinesiology cleared my mind and sharpened my focus so that I achieved far more in several months than I had managed in years before. A major plus is that Applied Kinesiology has proved to be a form of preventive medicine, which has raised my general health by improving my immune system and helping me cope with stress.

Dalcroze

Emile Jaques-Dalcroze, while Professor at Geneva Conservatoire, realised that many of his students, although technically proficient on their instruments, had difficulty playing in time and with rhythmic integrity. These problems remain a challenge to many young musicians today.

Paula Melville-Clark, lecturer at the University of Southern Queensland and president of Dalcroze Queensland describes the system of music education which he evolved:

Dalcroze became disillusioned with conventional approaches to teaching music and began to develop an approach based on the links between body and mind. He established a form of rhythmic movement called Eurhythmics, based on the premise that rhythm is the primary element of music and that the natural rhythms of the body act as the source of any musical rhythmic experience.

Dalcroze combined this with instruction in ear training (solfège) and improvisation. He found that when he got his students to move and respond to musical elements, they performed them with greater accuracy and with a sense of the underlying flow of the music. In other words, moving to the music helped them to understand the essence of the music, not just in terms of precision but also of expressive interpretation. These elements are essential to a proficient, effective and confident performance.

Feldenkrais

Respected physicist Dr Moshe Feldenkrais faced a series of operations, wheelchairs and lifelong dependency after sports injuries had caused him great pain. He applied his knowledge of various sciences and martial arts to experiments on the connection between mind and body.

His resulting system of body awareness and sequential movements has given relief to many suffering from repetitive strain injury, painful injuries and neurological disorders such as strokes. It also improves coordination and a sense of general wellbeing.

Mental imaging

Program your dreams. See yourself succeeding. An important part of the build-up to a performance is the mental preparation. Sit or lie comfortably relaxed and undisturbed while you visualise yourself sailing successfully through the program.

See yourself walking calm and poised onto the platform, opening your mouth to sing or speak, lifting hands to the keyboard or raising the bow. Hear the vibrant tone that flows out. Out of the corner of your eye, do you see those fear-gremlins skulk away into the shadows at the back of the stage, whilst you are encompassed in the warm, flattering and protective stage light?

Ah, here comes that tricky passage you worked through so thoroughly in rehearsal. Feel those relaxed fingers and shoulder muscles as you smoothly negotiate the pitfalls. Feel the exhilaration.

Do you notice how the faces in the audience respond to you, smile up at you? Hear them clapping, shouting 'Bravo!' See yourself bowing graciously, being wooed back onstage for more curtain calls, see the applause demand an encore. See yourself backstage with your diary open, wondering where you can find time for a repeat performance …

If you can visualise yourself in this positive light, you are well on the way to fulfilling all your hopes and dreams. Repeat positive affirmations to yourself. Some possibilities are:

- **'It is enough that I strive for excellence rather than perfection.'**

- 'I allow myself to feel nervous, vulnerable or fearful and I ask for the help and support that I need.'
- 'I will enjoy this performance, mistakes and all.'
- 'I accept that it is enough for me to do my best.'
- 'I allow myself to make mistakes, but I keep going.'
- 'I enjoy these beautiful, singing phrases. My audience enjoys my music.'
- 'I enjoy playing this beautiful music as expressively as I can.'

Barbra Streisand proved the success of mental imaging. As a child she spent much time alone imagining herself as various movie heroines:

Whenever I tried to imagine my future, I ran into a blank wall. I couldn't see kids or a husband or a home. I couldn't imagine any of the normal things.

(*Streisand; The Woman and the Legend*, James Spada, p. 22)

Instead, she imagined great things – fame and fortune. Her fantasies were all-encompassing. She would be a famous actress and the greatest star.

Hypnotherapy

Hypnosis is similar to mental imaging and can be a useful tool for combating onstage nerves. Various techniques of self-hypnosis can be learned from a qualified practitioner for general relaxation and stress reduction, or for the more specific purpose of reducing performance anxiety. We need to feel sure we are in the hands of a competent and trustworthy practitioner.

In self-hypnosis, one feeds positive, uplifting and encouraging instructions to the subconscious 'automatic' mind, the part of the mind on which one relies during performance. If the subconscious mind is not trained to cope with the increased stress levels experienced in challenging situations, then the performer has nothing to fall back on when overcome by a sudden anxiety attack.

During a process of hypnosis, the conscious mind is 'put to sleep' or 'lowered' and the subconscious mind is 'raised' to a level of seeming consciousness in order to be given instructions. As a negatively worded suggestion will illicit a negative or confused response, it is important always to give positive instructions, such as:

- **'My fingers are relaxed, move freely over my instrument.'**
- **'I feel calm and poised.'**
- **'I am filled with inner strength and vitality.'**
- **'I feel a warm rapport with the audience. I enjoy playing to them.'**

Merely thinking a keyword often helps the subconscious to respond. An instruction such as 'I carry myself with poise' can be condensed to the keyword 'poise', producing confidence and calm, as clarinettist Michaela Nathan can vouch:

My main keyword 'poise' helps me in the moments before I walk on stage and in the few seconds before a performance. I find that other instructions linked to the word come into my mind and my whole body feels immediately poised and relaxed and confident.

Before I started using this, I used to feel as if I wasn't there, not in my body, and I couldn't focus. Using hypnotherapy increased my focus, centred my energy and put me 'back into my body'. It also increased my rapport with the audience; I don't feel intimidated by them now.

Stretching and yoga exercises

Many of the above systems focus on the fact that stressed people tend to hunch in on themselves as a defensive mechanism. Various systems of yoga, Alexander Technique and Brain Gym offer useful exercises to counter this instinctive tendency. The stretching and lengthening of the spine is highly beneficial.

Offload stress with a good cry or laugh

Crying releases emotions that choke us. They may include excitement as well as grief or disappointment. Accept this therapy and do not feel ashamed of tears. Another advantage is that with the tears go potentially harmful chemicals produced during stressful times.

Laughter is a medicine. Smiling positively changes body chemistry and physiology. Whereas a frown increases downward jaw pressure onto the larynx, a smile uplifts with its upward muscular thrust. When we laugh, our zygomatic muscle contracts, sending increased blood to our brain. As blood pressure consequently rises and falls, the brain receives an oxygen bath similar to that from a short exercise workout.

We must never take ourselves so seriously that we cease to see the humour in situations. People have actually cured themselves of illnesses by hiring piles of funny videos and literally laughing themselves to health.

Progressive relaxation

With the adrenaline coursing through the body it is not really possible or advisable to be hyper-relaxed when on stage. A tennis player or violinist cannot afford to be so relaxed that they would drop the racquet or bow. The time to seek relaxation is not when under pressure, with the body in a state of heightened arousal. Save that for the day after, lolling in the sun with a book.

In performance we need, rather, a manageable minimum of tension and that in the right places, not overall. We need the elasticity of a rubber band which is pliable, stretching this way and that with resilience, but does not flop back loosely.

So, how do we relax? Admonishing performers to 'Relax!' often has the opposite effect. Far better, the words 'Let go!' Relaxation must be a passive, rather than busy search; the harder we try, the less we achieve true relaxation. When we go into the 'try' mode, we primarily use the left hemisphere of the brain. As the right side is more receptive, we need to integrate both sides. Meditation is one effective way of relaxing.

Meditation

Many people vouch for meditation techniques to calm and focus thoughts and concentration and to enhance energy. There are various courses, books and tape recordings which take the listener through stages of relaxing the muscles of the body progressively, and then continue with mental imagery.

The Eastern tradition is to empty the mind, not only of troubles and concerns, but of all awareness. This requires considerable training and may leave it open for less productive input. Most Westerners prefer to divert attention to a specific focus, like breathing or muscular tension. Others find it easier to imagine a safe, peaceful scene.

David Axten, counsellor and lecturer at the Queensland University of Technology, says:

> *The trick is not to fight thoughts, but to acknowledge them and let them go. For example, imagine writing them in the sand and letting the waves wash them away.*
>
> *One of my favourites is to write a keyword in my imagination, place it on a leaf and let it float away downstream. If the thought returns, repeat the process to let it go.*

Biofeedback

A simplified version of biofeedback is a technique where you may rate your body tension on a scale of one to ten. Choose an aspect for improvement – shoulder or neck tension, perhaps. Rate the tension of this part on a scale of one to ten. Consciously try to worsen the problem, noting which muscles tighten. Relax those muscles. When performing under stress, recall and repeat the sensation of letting go these muscles.

Some find it helpful, when exaggerating a tension point by tightening muscles further, to imagine that tension as a colour. Let that imaginary colour fill the whole place. Give it a sound, a texture. In changing channels of perception, we move as in a dream. We discover our edge, our fear boundary, and look beyond it in safety.

Interpersonal process recall

Another technique used by psychotherapists, formulated by Norman Kagan, uses video recall as a means of learning from any experience, including uncomfortable emotions during performance.

The performer watches a video replay from the safe distance of having 'lived to tell the tale'. The therapist does not criticise the performance, but rather acts as an inquirer to help the artist to explore thoughts, emotions, hopes, fears and body reactions that surface to awareness while watching the replay. Pause for every awareness, no matter how trivial, and ask questions such as:

- **What were you thinking at that point?**

- **What should you feel?**
- **Where in your body did you feel it?**
- **What did you hope/fear?**
- **What were the risks for you?**

Reprogramming past traumatic experiences

Several alternative approaches have emerged in psychotherapy which enable people to diminish the degree of inhibition and discomfort experienced after a traumatic experience. This may be related to a particularly bad performance, perhaps when young, or the diminished esteem and increased anxiety that comes from any unprocessed bad experience. Techniques that have helped performers include:

Eye movement desensitisation and reprogramming (EMDR). This technique has been pioneered by Dr Francine Shapiro and is the fastest-growing preferred way of dealing with past traumas which continue to affect people adversely. It is based on the discovery that traumatic memories remain locked in one segment of the brain. Rapid eye movement seems to shift the memory to other sections of the brain, creating new pathways. The person who has experienced trauma is asked to recall the memory and to move their eyes, following the therapist's finger.

David Axten again:

In this way, a traumatic memory can be very quickly reprocessed as the person knows they have survived the event. They often realise that a childhood trauma such as parental divorce, death of a close person or sexual abuse was not their fault. They did the best they could and are often freed from inappropriate subconscious guilt which erodes confidence. I have seen symptoms of severe post traumas relieved very rapidly for many people by this simple technique.

The patient is asked to recall the traumatic memory and to move their eyes, following the therapist's finger. In this way, the uncomfortable memories are filed away in a less accessible part of the brain. In many cases, even severe trauma has been greatly improved in a relatively short session. This technique has been used with Vietnam veterans.

116

Neuro-linguistic programming.

This offers mental tools to distance players from unpleasant memories. There are several variations, including: Recall the feeling of a performance or other situation which was upsetting to you. Remember the setting, the time and atmosphere, your dress, the sounds. Relive the horrors.

Imagine that your performance was videotaped and you are watching it on a screen. Play the tape at double speed so that the figures scurry across the screen. Now at triple speed, quadruple speed: laugh at how they trip over themselves in their eagerness. Then press the rewind switch and make them run backwards, in slow motion. Now watch yourself objectively as if from the stalls, a member of the audience, or as if watching yourself on television – both the serious and the fun versions.

This process defuses the tense memories by reframing your outlook on the event. It also offers several mental tools to distance yourself from an upsetting event or to highlight desired goals. For example, you can distance yourself from an unpleasant memory by imagining yourself watching it on a screen. Then sit a row further back and observe yourself watching the screen. Go back another row, and another until you are distant from the picture. Imagine all these watchers leaving, starting with the one closest to the screen until only you, most distant, are left. Imagine the picture being rewound fast, perhaps with light carousel music, before switching off the set and leaving.

Another common technique: Replace a feared image with an image of success. Make it bigger and brighter on the screen of the mind. Practise swapping from one image to the other, so that the undesirable image can be quickly replaced.

Cognitive behavioural therapy

A counsellor may use approaches that challenge our way of thinking and change behaviours in order to identify thought patterns that cause problems, walking us through them in a non-threatening way. In our imagination, we can approach our feared situations in gradual steps, staying relaxed. We can create the steps ourselves, from the easiest to the most difficult goal. Each step can then be taken and reinforced before moving on.

As well as approaching change in imagination, we may link the change with small steps in reality. For example, it may be easier to play to one person who is supportive, then before a friendly small group, then a group of strangers, of critics, or in a larger, more formal concert.

Brisbane teacher Hilary Yates describes her experience of this:

All your core beliefs are formed in the first five years of life. Core beliefs can be irrational. Cognitive behaviour therapy teaches you to challenge those irrational core beliefs and to replace them with rational ones, at both behavioural and emotional levels. If you are in a depressed state, it helps to have someone discuss these thoughts and to help sort them out. I used to apologise endlessly in rehearsals, but the therapy has given me confidence, so I now feel I can take on the world!

Overcoming adrenaline fatigue

The adrenaline rush is a potent force and needs to be managed in the performer's life. Ann Bachman, bass player with The Queensland Orchestra, learned to factor in the letdown of adrenaline after performances:

After a concert, you feel great, really high. I find when the adrenaline's pumping, you're not sensitive to when you've had enough. But I came to dread Sunday mornings! I would be so tired I could hardly drag myself out of bed. I'd feel flat … bad headaches …

I now find breathing exercises (especially inhaling and exhaling to an even count) and stretching and some yoga balancing exercises really help. We should let down our adrenaline by going out and doing something physical, like dancing. But many musicians tend to just go to the bar and drink a lot. That's probably the worst thing to do. Now, before I go to bed, I do shoulder stretching and deep breathing to slow down my mind. I wake up feeling much more positive and relaxed.

As performers, many of us are constantly on the run, performing every night, with little time to catch up on our thoughts, let alone sleep or energy. We have stoked up our adrenaline so constantly that we reach adrenal fatigue; we suffer burn-out. In this exhaustion phase, our immune system is so severely depleted that it is not surprising if we fall ill. Psychologically, also, physical illness may be our only way of stopping the hurdy-gurdy. 'Stop the world, I want to get off' is a phrase that typifies such exhaustion.

My chiropractor/kinesiologist helped me in such a phase by treating the neurolymphatic pressure points at the base of the ribs on either side of the spine near the kidneys (known as T11 and T12). Ask a friend to massage this area or to gently press down for a few seconds on this point. With this and Rescue Remedy drops I regained strength and coped far better with the challenges.

Prayer

Taking centre-stage can be a lonely place, even amongst other players. We all sometimes feel vulnerable and alone up on stage. We all need some individual form of personal belief to comfort and strengthen us at such times, to know we are not alone. Prayer is even more effective than meditation; not only does it calm our breath, mind and spirit, it draws on power outside ourselves, beyond our own limited means.

Some form of spiritual belief is necessary to balance the impersonal jungle of a technological age. Even if we address God by different names, such as a 'Power greater than ourselves', most of us recognise that we cannot manage alone.

We can draw on this power through prayer.

How do we pray? We may pray anywhere – on-stage, backstage, on the run … Even 'God, help me' is a prayer.

However, remember that last-minute 'gimme' prayers are those least likely to attract miracles. The Biblical saying 'You reap what you sow' is all too true. If the solid preparation is not done, it is hardly reasonable to expect a miracle cure to zap our tongue, vocal folds or fingers because of a last-minute prayer.

Sydney violinist Perry Hart told how her mother instilled in her the realisation that her talent was God-given:

My Mum would pray with me before a performance: 'Please, God, let Perry play as well as she has practised and remember that she didn't do it alone.' I used to mutter inside, 'But it wasn't God that did all that practice!' Now, looking back, I bless my mother because she put it into proportion: I only did the practice, but the gift was given to me. Our job is to use the gift wisely, responsibly ... or not. We can choose what we do as it's a gift, not a right.

The most effective form of praying percolates through our thought processes as we go about our daily life any time, any place. As blood sends nutrients and energy all through our bodies, brain and nervous system, so, when in touch with this power, prayer permeates our whole being.

This calming, steadying communication with God, ideally ongoing and regular, enables us to achieve the best results possible, rather than seek a random flash of brilliance. It is most valuable as a developing process, rather than a sudden miracle.

Sit down quietly, uninterrupted, with your score or part. Think it through, asking for help with specific problems, for calm and clarity of mind here, strength or conviction there, sure fingers in that tricky passage. Continue the conversation as you practise.

Such prayer steadies nerves which could block us, gives us conviction and confidence, clears our head of the clutters of self-doubt or panic. It enables us to do our best, to be open to communicate with others. It renews our enthusiasm in our work. In asking for help to develop those God-given talents, we can discover far greater potential in ourselves than we realised we possessed.

Enthusiasm is a powerful force, an often underestimated secret of success. A clue lies in its derivation from two Greek words, *en*, meaning 'in' and *theos*, meaning 'God' – literally, 'God in you'. This 'God-power' can be released within us through dynamic prayer, to enable us to accomplish those performances and high standards to which we aspire, probably even far beyond our expectations!

But what if my prayer is not answered?

Often, we may feel that there is no response to our prayer. Even saints have known this bewildering doubt.

'Ask and you shall receive.' Unfortunately, we tend to be impatient. We presume that a prayer is unanswered because it is not answered right now, today, when we need it. We give up too easily. Perhaps God has been answering all along, taking His own good time, and the mastery we hoped for today will be noticed next week or next month. It may be answered in a way different to our expectations.

One common reason for unanswered prayer is lack of faith. Rather than give up when a prompt miracle fails to fire our voice or fingers, we need to ask and go on asking to gain results.

Do I hear you say, 'But I don't know that I believe in God, so how can I pray?' Never mind. Perhaps you cannot put a name to the source of power, but you believe in something. That's a start. Jesus Christ said, 'I assure you that if you have faith as big as a mustard seed ... you could do anything!' That is enough for him to hear and answer. Try it; you have nothing to lose.

Philip Farkas was unnerved by negative thinking when he found himself catapulted into the principal horn chair of the Chicago Symphony Orchestra at the age of twenty-two. He admits he was not ready for this, neither age-wise nor experience-wise. His panic calmed with this realisation:

> *I was led there by an amazing chain of events, not just mere*
> *coincidence and, because I had been led there, certainly I could*
> *do the work assigned to me. I was now there because it was*
> *planned for me and failure was not part of that plan.*
> (*The Art of French Horn Playing*, Philip Farkas, p. 50)

Before each performance, Farkas read this page which he found inspiring and confidence-building:

> *I am in my right place*
>
> *The Lord will perfect that which concerns me ... (Psalm 138:8)*
>
> *... I am here where the One has placed me, doing what he has*
> *given me to do, in the way he has shown me to do it. When it*
> *needs to be done in new ways, he will prompt me to do it in his*
> *way. All results are in his hand; therefore, I will rejoice in what I*
> *do and bless the way it is done ... He will instruct and teach me in*
> *the way I shall go; he will guide me with his eye.*
> (Anita Scofield, Religious Science International, California.)

Some prayers for performers:

God be in my head and in my understanding.

God be in my eyes and in my looking.
God be in my mouth and in my speaking.
God be in my ears and in my hearing.
God be in my fingers and in my fluency.
God be in my heart and in my thinking.
God be at my end and at my departing.

The Lord be with us to guide us,
Within us to strengthen us,
Without us to protect us,
Above us to raise us,
Beneath us to uphold us,
Before us to lead us,
Behind us to guard us,
Even about us, this day and unto life everlasting
Amen. Thanks be to God.

(Source unknown)

Summary

- **All performers, whatever their instrument, benefit from focus on deep breathing. This calms excess adrenaline rush and also enables the music to flow.**
- **When challenged in a performance situation, posture instinctively hunches. A natural, upright stance enhances projection and tone production.**
- **Simple actions such as walking (cross-crawl), stretching, yawning and drinking plenty of water enable whole-brain expression.**
- **Performers can find encouragement, clarity and poise through progressive relaxation techniques, mental imaging, meditation, cognitive thinking methods and prayer.**

Part C

Specific situations

9

Problems and solutions for musicians

*Hermstedt … who always when appearing in public went to work
with the most nervous precision in everything, emboldened now to
rashness by the fumes of the champagne, had screwed on a new
and untried plate to the mouthpiece of his clarinet … Just as he
was about to increase [the volume] to its highest power, it gave
out a mis-tone resembling the shrill cry of a goose. The public
laughed, and the now sobered virtuoso turned deadly pale with
horror.*

(*Autobiography*, Louis Spohr, p. 156)

MUSICAL PERFORMERS ENCOUNTER various practical
problems, some common to many, others specific to their particular
instruments. These may cause acute discomfort, enough to
considerably increase nervous strain. We can prepare for such
difficulties by discovering how others cope with them. Conductors
may be more sympathetic or able to help their players if primed.

Common problems and solutions for musicians

All instrumentalists can be affected by shakes, intonation
difficulties and perspiration.

The shakes

A paradoxical approach often works here. Rather than fight against
shaking, give yourself permission to do so. Try to increase the
shaking, thinking 'So, you want to shake, fingers. Well, go on, shake!
Let's get it over with.'

Another tactic is to focus your attention elsewhere, away from
those shaky fingers. This was proved by a student at an American

summer music program, John Allegar, a talented organist and clarinetist. In our coaching session he admitted to suffering every symptom possible when performing. Soon after his session, he performed creditably. I congratulated him on his poise and calm; if he experienced any jitters they certainly were not obvious to the audience. 'Oh,' he said, 'I did have shaky hands in the beginning, then I remembered what you said and focused on my toes. But then they started to shake a little. So I brought my attention back onto my hands, and by then the piece was over.'

Jittery fingers may be a product of tense muscles or of too much energy as a result of the adrenaline rush. Before going on-stage, vigorously shake your fingers and jump or run on the spot to ease wobbly legs. Similarly, squeeze your fingers into a tight fist, then release.

Another solution is to direct our thoughts onto another aspect of our performance. Our minds just cannot think of two things at once. We can deliberately choose to focus on our strengths instead of weaknesses like shaking.

The intonation bogey

It is possible to panic when tuning-up or to become so anxious that we cannot distinguish intonation at all. Consequently, we may lose confidence in our hearing ability.

Sit down calmly, well before a performance and practise tuning to a piano or other instruments. Softly sing the notes out aloud. If you are uncertain as to whether a note is sharp or flat, listen for the 'beats' caused by sound waves. A slow 'wow wow' wave will speed up to a faster 'wah wah' as tuning becomes closer, then merges into the note. Exaggerate a note's sharpness or flatness, then gradually diminish it until the beats merge.

Many musicians rush when nervous and so have little time to listen acutely. Singers, trombonists and string players are particularly challenged by tuning as they must pitch all the notes by ear. The latter are especially prone to rigidity in the left-hand fingers, thumb and wrist due to the necessarily extreme leftward twist of the hand. Although the lower strings do not experience this twist, they also struggle with pitch problems as a result of rigidity.

Remember that tuning is a flexible matter in which one is sharper or flatter, rather than 'right' or 'wrong'. Listen carefully to the accompanist or other musicians. It helps to realise that the word 'intonation' centres around 'tone' that is, 'in-ton-ation'. If we listen to create a beautiful tone rather than focus only on tuning, the latter is often instinctively adjusted.

That instinctive nervous tendency to contract into a defensive, foetal position when threatened means that many players sharpen in pitch. Singers, wind and brass players tighten muscles of the throat, jaw, lips. Throat tension and pinching on the reed or mouthpiece squeeze out a choked thin sound, upsetting the air stream. The player tries to compensate by playing louder, which worsens the problem.

Throat restriction also tightens up the neck and shoulder muscles, limiting the use of the upper limbs. Concentrate on your diaphragmatic control to lessen this.

When pressured, string players tend to constrict arms and raise shoulders, so the fingers cramp closer together, sharpening the pitch. As violinists cannot fully see the fingerboard, some develop a mental block that this is longer than it actually is and that the fingers have further to travel in certain positions.

Perspiration problems

Many musicians struggle with slippery, sweaty fingers. This is hazardous to string players' intonation, making position shifts tricky and fine motor adjustments less acute.

The string players of the Baroque era had a ready answer for the hazards of sweaty fingers – they ran their fingers through the powder in their wigs. Today's prepared musicians may keep talcum power in their cases. Spraying fingers with antiperspirant before playing is a dubious solution because chemicals may adversely affect wooden instruments. Some guitarists spray a mild lubricant onto instruments to prevent stickiness.

Rather than worry about the sweating itself, try to lessen the causes of sweating – that is, increased adrenaline flow via the flight or fight mechanism.

Problems and solutions for string players

The acclaimed Belgian violinist Eugéne Ysaÿe struggled with *le trac*, which often caused bow trembling. The renowned pedagogue Carl Flesch attributed this in part to a faulty bow-hold; Ysaÿe used to hold his bow with an iron-tight grip between the thumb and three fingers while the little finger was always lifted off the stick, instead of balancing the bow. Ysaÿe wrote: 'The fingers are weak and the bow unsteady ... I am going through one of those pessimistic crises, nerve-racking and terribly sad ... I battle the crisis, I preach to myself, but until now the crisis overcomes me.' (*Great Masters of the Violin*, Boris Schwarz, p 282)

It is not surprising that many violinists and violists fear dropping their instrument or bow. They are challenged by the sheer impracticability of an often ungainly posture and the physics of holding their musical instrument between chin and shoulder. This may result in a 'bent coat-hanger' posture being adopted by those of tall physique. My tall violinist husband used to suffer agonies of backache. After considering his posture and balance through the Alexander Technique and yoga exercises, he coped with the rigorous three-call days of the London freelance scene.

Fear of dropping the instrument

Many violinists and violists who fear dropping the instrument or bow grip too firmly, cramping neck, shoulder and chin. Shoulder tension is especially common because of the need to hold the violin under the chin; many exaggerate the head pressure on the chin rest. If a tender lump develops on the neck, this means the player is gripping too hard and too often. Apply methylated spirits to the lump to harden and desensitise it. It is important to learn to hold the neck lightly.

Drawing up the left shoulder excessively and unnaturally causes immense fatigue and prolonged abuse results in chronic arm trouble. Many players are afraid to venture into higher positions and so faulty intonation and tense vibrato result. Balance the instrument so that the shoulder supports eighty per cent of the weight of the instrument and the left hand the other twenty per cent.

The fear of dropping the violin is exacerbated by a rigid stance caused by the feeling of an abyss underneath the instrument, according to Kato Havas, whose own experiences of stage fright prompted renowned books and courses on the topic. Her solutions include a comfortable stance with knee-bend motion and balance, generating an organic rhythmic pulse from the body itself. She eliminates the bogey of the 'violin-hold' by treating the instrument as a live weight instead of a dead weight.

Bow shakes usually occur on the downward stroke rather than the upward, where the sense of lifting is an active thrust rather than falling momentum. With the upward swing, one uses the third finger to push into the eye of the bow. If the same feeling can be captured on the down bow, it can alleviate the shakiness. Try drawing the bow faster.

Apply more weight into the string with a relaxed arm. German violist Ulrike Reutlinger advises: 'I prefer to begin a solo recital with a strong forte movement. As the right hand must execute heavy actions, this overrides any quivering or shaking.'

My husband says: 'It helps to raise the right elbow more and try to apply weight on the bow using the right-hand ring finger. Rather than projecting the sound down into the instrument, think of lifting it out of the instrument with the bow. This principle is similar with both violins and celli.'

The eminent violin pedagogue Carl Flesch advised to press down the stick with an increased outward turning of the lower arm in the elbow-joint,

> ... whereby the sources of strength are transferred from hand and fingers to the upper and lower arm. Though usually rejected as a waste of strength, many violinists prevent trembling of the hand by means of a wave-like vertical or horizontal movement of the arm.
> (*The Art of Violin Playing*, Carl Flesch, p. 88)

The violinist Yehudi Menuhin summed up the problems:

> A major fault in young violinists is the conviction that they and their violins must be riveted together. Their left hands, firmly grasping the instrument, cannot move to play it. Their stiff necks and rigid heads, braced arms and shoulders are so many fences between them and freedom. I have sympathy for them because I remember what it was like. My own mistake as a beginner was to

tuck away the fourth finger of my left hand, like a guest not
wanted at this particular party. To release young muscles from
bondage, it is my practice ... to invent a thousand curious
exercises. I make a child roll the neck of a violin between thumb
and fingers to loosen that desperate clutch.

(*Unfinished Journey*, Yehudi Menuhin, pp. 484-5)

The cellist's natural, seated posture is generally more comfortable than that of the violinist. However, the cellist's particular hazard is that the instrument's supporting spike may slip. It is important to invest in a good supporting board for this rather than trust little holes dug into the floor. Practical foresight, like checking that the spike is sharp and securely tightened before playing, can save embarrassing moments which are just bad luck, rather than a result of nerves. Cellist Juliet Hoey says: 'During a cello exam, the spike gradually retreated into the cello and I ended up hunched over the instrument like a gorilla.'

For cellists, retraction of the right arm back into the body under stress causes poor tone as the bow will not travel straight and retreats to a position over the fingerboard.

Viola players must support a longer, heavier instrument than the violin, which may cause discomfort. The eighty-twenty principle mentioned earlier in the chapter is of particular help to them. For this reason, tall players with lanky arms are often attracted to the instrument rather than those of smaller physique.

Violist Elizabeth Morgan says:

Often the type of people attracted to the viola are more deeply
philosophical personalities who may be more prone to
apprehensions. And then it's tricky because they're not often in the
limelight. The viola section is chugging along happily and they
suddenly fall off their chairs when they come to a solo because
they're not used to exposure.

Problems and solutions for guitar players

The guitar, whether used in rock, classical, country and western or whatever, has its problems. Classical guitarists with their very subtle sound are concerned either that the sound carries in the hall or, when recorded, that other extraneous noises don't carry all the more. Rock

129

guitarists with amplification may find themselves even more exposed when things go wrong.

Rock guitarist Peter Sinclair explains:

In an orchestra with fifty or sixty others, it doesn't matter so much if one makes a mistake. But in a rock band, there are only four or five of you. You have to be primed in case something goes wrong, like a string breaking.

Probably, you will feel it snap before you hear it. Muffle it with the right hand; signal to your roadie to throw that spare guitar through from the wings. Meanwhile, the drummer has snapped into a drum solo. Or you can do fun things to turn a negative into a positive, like the times I say: 'I've decided to do a breathing solo' and I huff into the mike. Everyone laughs, people think, 'Oh, they're having a good time – let's have another drink.' You do need to have several guitars on hold; otherwise, you have to stop and call a break sooner or later.

Apart from the risk of broken strings, fingernails are the bane of the guitarist's performing life, presenting an uneasy state of flux as they grow or split. Julian Bream worries whether a nail will be too long, short, brittle, or worse, chipped for the night of a performance:

Are my nails a bit on the long side? Is the sound a bit thin, so had I better play nearer the sound hole? ... if I get a bit run down or I've got the flu, then my nails get thin and, d'you know, the sound gets thin also and cold weather can make them brittle. Which is dangerous, as they are then liable to split.

(*A Life on the Road*, Julian Bream, pp. 36, 10)

Humidity may affect the acoustics:

Bream continues:

Is the humidity too dry, so [that] the string flexibility [is] too great? If the humidity is dry, the bridge sound [ponticello] will be unusually bright ... So now I've weighed up the acoustics of the hall and something of the quality of the audience. I'm pretty sure about how I'm going to set my tempi, because of the sound reverberation or lack of it; and according to how I'm feeling physically, I'll have some idea how I'm going to pace myself for the rest of the concert.

(*A Life on the Road*, Julian Bream, p. 10)

Projecting such a quiet instrument in a big auditorium is difficult, especially in live recordings, where the louder passages need full strength action, possibly to the point of distortion of sound. Bream points out that in a concert hall, such distortion is moderated by the time it reaches the listeners' ears:

> *But a highly sensitive condenser microphone can pick up that distortion, however faint it may be and, when I am making a recording, I am always aware of this. It therefore takes me time to relax and settle down … it may take an hour or longer sometimes before I can really begin to make music.*

> (*A Life on the Road*, Julian Bream, p. 8)

Problems and solutions for wind players

A bane of wind players is that condensation can accumulate under pads, producing embarrassing gurgling sounds on corresponding notes. Experienced wind players never venture on stage without cigarette papers to mop such leaks during rest bars.

Wind and brass soloists can gain a few minutes' breathing space between pieces or movements by cleaning out the drips from their instrument.

Reed players feel more confident if they make an opportunity to test their reeds in each varied acoustic before concerts. What appears ideal backstage may be over or under responsive in the auditorium. A very soft reed may be too exuberant, making it difficult to control the tone, whereas too hard a reed may require much greater exertion.

For clarinetists

While all musicians may express tension in unsettling ways, surely the clarinetist suffers the worst ignominity. No instrumentalists advertise their nerves so obviously as do clarinetists – with a loud squeak.

While misplaced, rigid fingers may be the culprits, tense pinching of the lips on the reed is the major cause. As a weed is just a plant growing in the wrong place, so a squeak is just a high note which will become part of the repertoire later. Such mishaps are quite normal in beginners. Even experienced professionals when tense may pinch on the reed and squeak. A few embarrassments may lead to squeakophobia. Fear of squeaking may inhibit air flow, causing a mousey, colourless and boring sound.

Even though overblowing may cause a few miscalculations, I encourage students to sing out with a positive, full tone, advising: 'If you do squeak, make it a good one!' Clarinetist Karlin Love advises her students 'to exaggerate the squeak, to make it squeak. And mostly they just can't do it!'

I have no qualms in admitting to pupils that I have squeaked in performance and, mercifully, forgotten it soon after. I have heard world famous clarinetists squeak in public and if it's okay for them, surely we can forgive ourselves an occasional 'canary'.

The solution to this problem is to relax lip and jaw pressure by buzzing lips in a 'raspberry' before walking on-stage, or with discreet yawning and 'teeth-rinsing' movements. Excess biting soon causes soreness of the inner lip where the teeth press in. A makeshift shield from cigarette papers or florists' tape gives some protection; or ask a dentist to make a dental guard. Check the mouth position: if too much bottom lip is tucked under, soreness is more likely. Unbalanced reeds may cause squeaks. Check also if too much mouthpiece is inserted in the mouth.

Second, finger problems. Fingers can move around musical instruments more freely when they are not desperately clutching them. (Tense violinists excessively grip instrument necks and bows.) The clarinet should balance on the right-hand thumb, with reinforcement from a secure mouth position. It is not necessary to 'hold' the instrument tightly. If weight is a problem, try a neck-strap which takes about fifty per cent of the weight from the vulnerable right-hand thumb. However, it is not an ideal solution, for the tension may be transferred to the neck muscles. One can obtain a neck-strap with waist support which bears all the weight, leaving fingers free.

For saxophonists

Saxophonists often lose control, both of vibrato and air column of the whole tube. They must develop a secure foundation of tone production.

Paul Harvey enlarges on this:

Uncontrolled vibrato, usually fast, uneven and emanating from the chest or twitching lips can be controlled by a regime of regular, even, measured vibrato practice. As soon as a student can sustain a good quality straight note with firm air support, vibrato can be introduced. This should be produced by the jaw (not the lips) moving up and down (not backwards and forwards). The more slow vibrato practice, the more control will be developed to prevent nervous vibrato.

Another symptom of nerves is excessive biting, causing thin, constricted tone and closing up of the reed. This can be cured by temporary remedial use of a double lip embouchure [mouth position] – for practice only, of course.

An added benefit of this treatment is that the airflow has to be increased, which exercises the diaphragm. Nerves are helped by deep breathing, so check that you are taking in air correctly when playing saxophone: drop the bottom jaw, keeping top teeth and lip against the top of the mouthpiece, and breathe in under the mouthpiece and reed as if absolutely horrified!

To prevent biting, consider an embouchure of a polite 'O', dropping the jaw. The lip is not as far over the bottom teeth this way, but more relaxed. This will cause less of a problem from sore lips. Because many saxophone teachers are primarily clarinetists, they tend to use a similar approach, but remember that a saxophone embouchure is much more relaxed than that of the clarinetist.

For flautists

A tense embouchure causes a thin, brittle sound and tense neck and shoulders can also affect the tone. Because flautists constantly move their mouth to adjust notes, shaking lips are a problem, affecting the direction of air flow. Consequently, tonal control is diminished; the lips can't relax enough to produce secure low notes and the soft dynamics are lost in the upper register. Rather than try to stop the shakes, it's better to think: 'So, lips, you're going to shake; well, go on and shake.'

Queensland flautist Jeanette Manricks offers these solutions: 'The secret is to build up the lip muscles with tone exercises like long notes, so they can still maintain control. As athletes train, so we must maintain peak condition. Shaky hands are less hazardous if we are totally familiar with our part and the more we perform the less likely they become.'

As with most wind instruments, breathing is often affected. A dry mouth can make tongue action and hence articulation less fluent and clear. Some suggestions for dealing with this are in Chapter 7.

Another problem involves the flute's headjoint. Flute teacher Frances Farmer suggests a solution:

Often when playing under stage lights, or just when nerves make
us perspire, the flute's headjoint slips against the chin. I suggest to
students that they attach a piece of chamois, an adhesive sticker or
stamp to the lip-plate where it comes in contact with the chin.

Some flautists reduce the risk of slipping by attaching postage stamps or resin; others engrave grooves into the head joint.

Resist the temptation to express your tension in a raised brow or locked jaw. Furrowed foreheads do not help embouchure; lifting eyebrows to play high or expressively really does not improve the actual pitch or sound. Ease this tension by gently massaging your fingers on your forehead, breathe easily, and soon you will feel calmness spreading over the area.

For oboists and bassoonists

Oboists often feel pent-up, pressured, even dizzy, as they must direct a limited air flow through the double reed's thin aperture. It is important to empty the lungs before inhaling again. Tension creates more problems for oboists, as David Nuttall, senior lecturer at the Canberra School of Music, Australian National University, notes:

If the embouchure is too tense, the low notes don't speak. We often
drop the air support when under pressure. Once that air vibration
drops below a certain speed, the reed just ceases to vibrate, so it
won't respond. With such a small reed, there is less margin for
error, so we tend to become more sensitive in everything we do.
The secret is to concentrate on a good embouchure, using the lip
muscles rather than the teeth and remember always to BLOW!

One often sees double reed players, especially oboists, scraping or moistening their reeds during rest bars. This indicates the scope of their problems. Dry reeds speak less reliably; add to this tension's dry mouth and a reluctant response is likely. Nerves may cause the player to pinch on the reed, sharpening pitch and thinning the sound.

The narrow oboe reed transmits a higher level of tension through the body, because the player's inner air pressure is also higher. 'I often can't form an embouchure before a solo because my throat tightens,' an oboist said. 'Then the first thing to go is the breathing and the sound becomes thinner because I tighten on the reed. Coffee, milk and meat seem to gum up my mouth, so I avoid them before playing.'

The bassoon reed is thicker and larger, so tension is less. However, any pinching of the reed causes a loss of dynamic range and control especially in the soft dynamics.

As with so many wind players, shallow breathing is a culprit. It causes players to compensate by pinching on the reed, producing a squeezed, tight sound.

Bassoonist Peter Musson suggests: 'Think low and concentrate on breathing deeply. I find that the Yoga Alternate Nostril Exercise helps steady the nerves and get the breathing going.'

As much of the standard repertoire is contained in the top third of the register, the full top octave consists of cross fingering, requiring secure preparation.

Problems and solutions for brass players

Brass players have to resign themselves to the fact that many music scores allocate them hundreds of rest bars. Suddenly, they are thrown into an important exposed solo. Serious players use these rest bars to 'psych' themselves up to pitch the sound of the first note in the inner ear, so that it comes automatically.

When a brass player shakes as a result of nerves, the vibrations are transferred back into the instrument. The answer is to centre this tendency with secure diaphragm control; and to relax the body and breathe slowly and deeply. Resist the temptation to tighten the throat, causing pitch to sharpen. The throat is just part of the pipeline between the diaphragm and the instrument.

A major worry, sore lips, can be avoided or alleviated by keeping in top form with regular practice and sensible warm-ups. Before performing, players should limber up gradually, without pressure. Nervous and out of form players exert excessive pressure on the lips, forgetting that the diaphragm support should take responsibility for about ninety per cent of the tonal control. However, Brisbane trumpeter Malcolm Liddell takes a slightly different tack:

> *I take the view that the movement of air, or 'air in motion', is more beneficial than concentrating on diaphragm and muscles. Young players constantly fall into the trap of 'over-analysing' their playing.*

Instead, their lips and aural cavity take over. The damage done in five minutes' squeezing might require twenty-four hours' rest to recover. Out-of-practice brass players often sport a red rim or crease around the lips. Good brass instrumentalists work to minimise pressure by maximising air flow, keeping body and facial muscles as relaxed as possible.

For trumpeters

An over-firm grip of the left hand on the valve casing while pulling unconsciously towards the lips indicates excessive tension. Inexperienced players may dig the little finger of the right hand into the finger-ring to lever it towards the lips and the higher the note, the more they pull.

Under these circumstances, pitch suffers also. When the lips tighten, control of intonation diminishes. In fact, it is the air velocity rather than the lips which controls pitch so there should be little change in embouchure throughout the range. The lips do control the pitch in a reactionary way: they react to how efficiently the air is passed through them into the instrument.

Posture is particularly important to trumpeters. The instrument is too heavy to hold up at the natural angle through which the column of air passes. Young players find the length of the instrument more of a problem than the weight. Also, the dental conformation overbite/underbite, or top teeth in relation to bottom teeth is a big factor in the instrument's playing angle.

For French horn players

Horn players have been described as 'independent cusses, who have to be able to be knocked down a hundred times and still smile'. The instrument demands an acute ear and skill as it tends to play predominantly high in the harmonic series where notes are close together. Even a tiny miscalculation caused by tense lips, tiredness, distraction, or even by moving the face slightly can cause a wrong note.

Acoustically, the horn's insertion of valves and tuning slides into a conically tapered tubing whose bore becomes progressively wider. This makes intonation difficult. This bore also presents more resistance to blow through than the trumpet family's straight-tapered tubing.

For trombonists

Kevin Brown, trombonist with the Queensland Symphony Orchestra, advises:

The trombone upper register can become thin or non-existent in performance stress situations. Try to play the challenging passage a third higher than required in the practice room to have confidence in playing the correct pitch in the performance.

He continues with an anecdote:

The bane of most trombonists is the solo in Ravel's Bolero. *Once the conductor asked me a few hours before the concert to play the solo. Although I had performed it before, on this occasion I was not prepared.*

Rather than practise it dozens of times, instead I opted to write down approximately thirty reasons why my Bolero would go well. These included statements like, 'I always sound so good playing this solo, and my rendition is always confident and correct, my high notes are played with ease and my rhythm is always true. People always comment how beautiful my Bolero *sounds, my tone fills the concert hall with ease, my breathing is steady and I'm well focused, etc'.*

I read and reread these statements many times and, again two minutes before my solo, I took the list from my tails jacket and reread the script. I was conditioning my mind for a good performance and on this occasion it did not let me down.

Problems and solutions for conductors

Imagine the damage to your car if you drove it for three hours with the handbrake on! Similarly, conductors who move arms which are locked at the joints because of tension may suffer intense shoulder and back pain.

It is important to remain flexible and relaxed, controlling the baton from the hand instead of the whole arm. Many inexperienced conductors need economy of action; save great dramatic gestures for climaxes and avoid duplicating actions by both hands, which merely wastes energy and clouds intentions.

Conductors must be physically fit to stand during performances of long works like Handel's *Messiah* or Wagnerian operas. Concentration is intense as the buck stops with the conductor if the ensemble wavers – a clear mind is essential. Ensure sufficient rest, increase water intake and avoid alcohol before performances.

Breathe deeply to maintain oxygen to the brain. Queensland Youth Orchestra Musical Director John Curro says:

I find I become tired very quickly if I don't breathe well. Also, you must have the structures worked out very clearly, the rhythmic and tempo transitions, section changes. You can't just hack away at the beats. Any conductor who stands in front of a group of people and expects them to help him get through makes a big mistake and deserves to get nervous.

Some conductors may fear dropping the baton. This causes them to grip harder, tightening arm muscles. It may help to know that this has happened to many others. Pablo Casals' baton went skittering off into the audience. Robert Schumann frequently dropped his baton. His novel solution was to tie it to his arm, saying, 'Look, now it can't fall again!'

What about shaky hands, raised for all to notice? This can be controlled by simply holding the tip of the baton in the other hand for a moment.

Conductors may lessen the fear of losing balance and falling backwards by using a podium rail, a device my husband, Antoni, found reassuring:

On the last night of a long, gruelling tour, I was tired, ill and somewhat disoriented. While conducting on an extremely high stage, I found myself hanging onto the conductor's stand for fear of falling backward.

In subsequent performances, I began to dread a recurrence of this uneasiness until I solved it by using a curved podium rail. I also had to psyche myself saying, 'I am in control of this situation and am responsible for these players.' If I couldn't do that, I might as well get off the stage.

Conductors may worry about losing their place in the score. It is essential to prepare thoroughly before rehearsals so as to be able to concentrate during rehearsals on string bowings, breathing points, tempo changes and transpositions.

Certainly, it helps to have sufficient rehearsal, but the hard economic reality is that many front the podium with far too little or none at all! Australian conductor Simone Young has often been called in to conduct Wagnerian operas without any rehearsal. When fellow conductor Charles Mackerras fell ill, Simone had two hours' notice to conduct Meistersingers in Munich:

I had the concertmaster's part waiting for me at the hotel when I arrived. I met with him and the singers to check my list of queries and had a short rehearsal with a small section of the chorus. Then, you can only go on, hoping they'll watch the beat. Plenty of rehearsal is the optimum, but there are times when none is available. I know that the quality of my own preparation pays off. I spend hours over the score. If there's time, I'll see a performance or a video if available, so I know what the orchestra is used to and can warn them of any tempi changes.

Problems and solutions for pianists

Pianists are fortunate in that they perform seated, so locked or shaky knees are less of a problem. They do not have to carry the weight of the instrument as do most other instrumentalists. Daniel Barenboim began playing the violin at three years of age, but when, a year later, he realised that the piano was supported by three legs, he quickly and successfully switched to that instrument.

However, pianists do sit relatively immobile for long hours of practice. Make regular opportunities to stretch and move other parts of the body. Unlike violinists who tend to grip the bow or wind players who clutch at keys, the pianists' tension is felt differently, for they are not actually holding on to keys. Finger and arm tension still need to be consciously released. Tension from the back and shoulders may be transmitted all down the arm to the wrist and fingers.

To counteract this, feel that you are playing all the way from the shoulder and not just the fingers. Before playing, relax with stretches, windmill and swing movements, and neck rolls. Lift your shoulders as high as possible, as if trying to touch your ears. While playing, remember to drop your shoulders; wiggle them unobtrusively between movements. Your more relaxed arms can then produce a fuller, better tone.

A major problem for pianists is that they are constantly forced to adapt to the eccentricities of foreign pianos and piano stools. Players develop an identity with their own instrument, practising according to its response. They then have to quickly assess and adjust to another instrument's touch.

It is especially important to arrive early before a concert to try out the instrument. If this is not possible, as in an eisteddfod, one must use the natural weight of the arm and sink the fingers into the keys to find the tonal scope of that instrument. Pianists must learn to judge quickly whether the action is excessively heavy or light. A heavy action makes fast passages more difficult. Yet it is usually recommended that young players practise on an instrument with relatively heavy action so that developing fingers are challenged.

Sandy Walker, Brisbane pianist and teacher, says:

To help my students manage playing on heavy action, I tell them to practise with the soft pedal on or with the practice pedal if they have one. If that's not enough, put both down. I train them to play their scales and technical work with high, marching fingers, while keeping the forearm and wrist level. They soon develop the ability to cope with a heavy touch. At every opportunity you can, play on heavy action pianos.

Pianist André Watts has this to say:

I get very impatient when I hear a violinist telling me his instrument 'isn't responding'. And I think, 'Hey, buddy, you're complaining about your own instrument when I've never even laid eyes on this monster in front of me!' ... When I arrive at the hall, I calmly gaze at it [a new 'monster'] for a long moment. This is my way of saying 'hello' to it. I never touch it right away.

But then I sit down to play and the piano reveals its qualities to me. Very quickly I find out if the bass is muddy or the treble is weak, and here begins my psychological adjustment to the instrument. I now have to make a choice. Will I be friends with the instrument or will I spoil a whole evening fighting with it?

In order to make friends, I must accept the weaknesses of the instrument. This is the state the piano is in. It's not trying to get you ... It's heartbreaking to realise that so many of the effects you have worked your guts out for will be lost. But there will inevitably be some place in the piece you're playing where a pianissimo will be aided by the weak treble; or where a blurry resonance will create a wonderful wash of sound.

So you must allow yourself to feel that somehow the piano will help you.

(*The World of the Concert Pianist*, David Duval, p. 326)

It is often said that everybody can play well on a good piano; the trick is to play well on a bad piano.

Program your recital to commence with a piece that you have performed many times in public. Then, having already played it on many different pianos, you are best able to adjust to the characteristics of the instrument. Before starting to play, place your foot on a pedal to discover if the stool is placed at the right distance from the instrument? It is too late to adjust this in the early bars of a piece.

Of such problems, Sandy Walker says:

Eisteddfods and auditions are minefields for the unprepared pianist – especially the short ones! Be ever vigilant regarding the nearest telephone, and check to see that a telephone book is nearby in case you need to increase the height of a broken piano stool!

To determine the right height of the piano stool for yourself, check that your forearm is parallel to the floor.

Check that the piano's wheel locks are secure. Pianist Carson Dron tells how once, 'playing Stravinsky's *Petroushka* in London, the piano started rolling away from me. I frequently had to move my stool to catch up with it.'

If performing in a competition, it's a tough prospect to follow a performer whose sweaty hands have made the keyboard slippery. Come primed with an extra handkerchief to wipe down the keyboard.

Pianists who accompany soloists are often under pressure to throw off thick clusters of chords while jumping beats or lines to catch the soloist's vagrant rhythm. They either scramble to turn their own pages in hectic pieces, or succumb to the mercies of itinerant page-turners, whose foibles are legion. There is the vacant eyed, lost-in-the-glorious-music (will he remember to turn or do I have to do it anyway?) or the one who, instead of following the score, fixes you with hawk-eyes for a nod, then still turns too late; or who misinterprets your body language and turns half a page early; or who scuffles with pages and licking fingers, then still manages to turn two pages at once.

The only solution is, when a difficult split-second timing work is scheduled, to organise a page-turner with whom you have worked already, one who understands how far ahead you read, who is discreet and unobtrusive and, above all, whom you can trust.

Problems and solutions for organists

Organists encounter many difficulties similar to those of pianists. As well, pipe organists may feel a sense of alienation, perched aloft on precipitous heights, with their back to the audience, feeling eyes boring into them.

Sylvia Blayse describes this sensation:

I used to feel their eyes on me as I perched insignificantly up there, battling the giant in order to produce gargantuan sounds. Is playing one of these monsters just a power trip? You ascend the precipitous bench, power on, loud subterranean wheeze, flaps open and take-off and sounds emerge which range from thunderous to celestial, all under the control of your shaky hands.

During a performance, I suddenly experienced a panic attack. I suddenly thought: 'I can't do this.' Then: 'Pull yourself together. Now!' The way I overcame it was to play the next couple of bars at

142

half-speed. I'm sure only the afficionados noticed and, strangely, they didn't make me anxious.

I think the relationship between performer and audience makes a big difference. Who made the rule that audiences must sit absolutely still and only cough if they will otherwise die, keeping rigid attention on the performer? Why the total lack of communication between performer and listeners, other than the stiff formal bow with eyes glazed? For me, performance anxiety would be considerably reduced if concerts were more user-friendly.

Summary

- **Each instrument has its challenges. Being well prepared lessens the angst. Be aware that many suffer similarly, and still present excellent performances.**

- **Give yourself permission to shake, and this will be less unsettling; focus on another part of your body, perhaps by wiggling your toes.**

- **Intonation is relative; there is no 'right and wrong' but rather 'higher or lower'. Focus on listening to produce a rounded tone and tuning will improve.**

- **Issues like excess perspiration, trembles, shakes, and squeaks are all by-products of tension and over-charged adrenaline. Focus on slow deep breathing channels the adrenaline into energy, and such issues may dissolve.**

10

How to handle that special opportunity

'Okay,' I'd think to myself, 'go ahead, shut the door in my face! Be out to lunch! Hang up on me! I don't care. I'll be back!' I was never intimidated by that sort of garbage, because I knew I was as good as anything else coming down the pike. I could sing. I could read lines.
Bette Midler (*Bette: An Intimate Biography of Bette Midler*, Georg Mair, p. 35)

WE HAVE SEEN WAYS TO HELP PLAYERS of various instruments cope with their particular problems. Now, let me walk you through specific situations that can involve stress, so that you can be more prepared. Picture yourself during the weeks before an event, coping with the particular stresses that such situations might bring.

There are a number of factors, some of which we have already mentioned, that can help us cope with auditions, competitions, recordings and examinations:

We know that nervousness will not be so daunting if we have prepared ourselves too much rather than too little. Even at the risk of complacence and a stale approach, we are ready, secure in our technique.

We have discussed with our teachers the standards required and have their confidence that our honest work of the past months can match these levels. With our teachers, we have chosen audition pieces which best show our strengths, whose demands we are capable of meeting and which are appropriate to the situation.

We have listened to recordings and concerts to gain an idea of style, but have thoughtfully developed our individual sound and

144

interpretation. We know the show's score and lyrics and something about the composer, style and period.

We have increased our confidence by playing in the venue beforehand, where possible, to 'feel' the acoustic and atmosphere. We telephoned the management last week to book the auditorium for a half-hour, knowing that it would be occupied on the day of the event. We checked the size of the stage, the lighting and the anticipated distance from ourselves to the audience or panel or microphone.

Then we invited a friend along, to advise on sound balance with the accompanist and whether the costume is right and projects a good image.

We have rehearsed with and brought along our own pianist rather than taking our chances in a cold run with one supplied by the organisation. We are comfortable with cues and ensemble.

We have checked with the management exactly what they want to hear so we can best meet their needs. We have chosen contrasting pieces that show our strengths.

We remind ourselves that although auditions and competitions may appoint only one winner, with little feedback, it is not really a win or lose, good or bad situation. Perhaps one of the jury will be impressed by our performance and remember us for a later position or production. Certainly, we will gain through this experience and present more competently next time.

We tell ourselves that to fail an audition or examination does not spell doom to a whole career. Others in the limelight have all had their failures as well as successes.

Guitarist Julian Bream wrote: 'I had never passed an examination in my life and always did appallingly badly in my exams at the Royal College. I had two auditions for BBC Radio, but failed both of them. So, I took any job that came my way' … eventually becoming a top performer on the international circuit.

Performance is unnatural in situations like examinations and auditions. Unlike during concerts, players cannot draw strength from the audience, sense their enjoyment and that most of them want us to succeed. Prepare for such unnatural sensations where you will be alone in a small studio with busily writing adjudicators, and realise that those written comments may be positive rather than negative.

Visualise … We are waiting in the warm-up room, having arrived in just enough time to comfortably unpack, do a few stretching and breathing exercises, warm up the voice or fingers, sit quietly and focus. Others may arrive late, hot and flustered, but we are calm. Nor have we sat around for an hour, our stomachs feeling more churned by the minute, fingers tangled from slashing fitfully at the semiquaver passages.

Sure, we touch up a few sections slowly, but as we have practised steadily for months, there is less urgency. As the adrenaline excites our systems we feel edgy – let's not be unrealistic! But basically we're calm, poised, raring to go.

All our equipment is organised. We've brought along spare reeds or strings, double-checked music (not like Chris over there, making a big fracas over the scores left at home on the piano) with tabbed pages to avoid fumbling. Singers and actors have vocalised and warmed up.

Auditions

'I was so nervous at the audition because it is the first time I've opened my mouth to sing in front of anyone but my dog,' said Renee Zellweger of her successful audition for the lead role in the film version of *Chicago*. Presumably the presentation skills she learned through other earlier auditions carried her through. As about ninety per cent of actors and singers at any time are 'resting' in temporary employment such as taxi-driving, they have to face frequent auditions in order to gain a future role on stage, television, film, or radio. 'Open' auditions for musicals are more commonly known as cattle calls. Here, hundreds of hopefuls are herded on stage in small groups, with a bare minute to make a memorable impression.

Even for modest chorus roles, it is worth presenting our stunning best. It is possible for a star to emerge from such inauspicious beginnings. An unknown university student auditioned for the chorus of *The Pirates of Penzance*, 'basically just to see what an audition was like'. But after several recalls, Marina Prior was cast in the lead role.

Looking back, she thought her inexperience helped rather than hindered. 'I had no idea what to expect, so I had a naive arrogance and I didn't load the situation as you do when you have more experience.' (Jo Litson, *Risky Business*, The Australian Weekend Review, October 23-4, 1996, p.10)

We can approach an audition creatively as yet another performance, perhaps even dare a few risks in order to be noticed. Another unknown initially irritated her panel by breaking all the rules. She rushed in, wearing an eccentric raccoon coat and odd shoes, explaining she was late because she had seen these marvellous shoes in a thrift shop and only one of each pair fitted. After stopping and starting, placing her chewing gum under a stool, she finally began to sing. The panel later discovered that there was no chewing gum – that this, the coat and shoes, were all part of a gambit to stand out from the crowd. Soon after, Barbra Streisand starred in *Funny Girl*. (Such tricky ploys are not to be recommended for orchestral auditions, where the management wants reliable players who will not arrive late for performances!)

Will we find auditions as harrowing as the show *A Chorus Line* presents? Singer Renee Fleming suffered low self-esteem after an early debut debacle in Salzburg and consequently didn't audition well. Her teacher, Beverley Johnson, recommended she visit a therapist, who pointed out that Fleming tended to visualise audiences and judges as negative. She convinced her that 'even in an audition, people don't want you to fail. They want to hear someone great'. This improved attitude bore results; a year later Fleming won the Metropolitan Opera's national auditions and the George London Prize in the same week, and joined the Houston Opera as a company member. (*Diva; The New Generation*, Helena Matheopoulos, p. 42.) Speaking on a recent ABC interview, Fleming said: 'At times I had a problem with performance, seeing audiences as a threat. I read books, took seminars, and worked on my way of thinking. I also worked on my technique, so I could trust myself.'

Melbourne singer and teacher Kathryn Sadler advises her students always to have prepared five pieces ready to go at any one time, because auditions often come at short notice: two uptempo pieces from different eras, two ballads from different eras and a character song:

> *Choose material that can be cut if it's too long and don't do repeats. There is no such thing as an audition piece that is too short! Audition panels generally know exactly what they're looking for and quite often make a decision within a few bars. The 'call-back' is the place for extended performance and usually the panel will ask for something specific.*
>
> *In the first round, be sure that the pieces demonstrate vocal range and, if possible, a variety of technical skills. Early music theatre (Cole Porter/Gershwin) is a great resource in this respect, because the songs often start with a slow 'verse' (demonstrating legato line), followed by a jaunty uptempo refrain (demonstrating articulation and often characterisation). They are short or, if they are not, they are easy to cut.*
>
> *Be sure that chosen pieces are in the correct key, which often may mean a complete transposition. Don't assume that the audition pianist will be happy with a mere transposition of the chord chart. Well-prepared, clearly marked sheet music is as important as the well-prepared performance. Do not choose material that is currently popular or has enjoyed a history of popularity. No matter how good the piece, no matter how well it is sung, the singer sets themselves up to be compared with other competitors – worse still, with famous singers who have brought the song its popularity.*

Choose a variety of audition material, geared to show contrasting facets of your abilities.

Orchestral musicians present two contrasting movements of a concerto and some sight-reading excerpts from their instrument's standard orchestral repertoire. Sight-reading may be asked 'on the spot' or prepared for a few days. We feel more confident if in recent months we have studied orchestral excerpts from available books and heard recordings to understand their style and place in the overall work.

An orchestral audition panel includes the concertmaster, general manager, the section leader of our own instrument and possibly the chief conductor. Casting agents handle acting and musical auditions, probably with the director and producer present.

So here we are, confronting a panel of experts lined up at the table, who write or confer busily in mutters and whispers, even laughs throughout. We speak politely when spoken to, but resist the temptation to show our nerves with time-wasting chatter or a weather report. We try to turn the performance into a concert in our head.

Even though we realise time is short, this does not mean we should allow ourselves to be rushed into the opening bars. Those twenty seconds required to poise ourselves on the launching pad are crucial and we have a right to these in order to play our best.

My husband auditioned for a German orchestra that offered three positions. They heard fifty applicants in an hour. Half a minute's playing, then the bell. Next, please. This reinforces earlier comments about the necessity to project those opening sounds with poise, confidence and positive tone. First impressions are enormously important. Singers may choose to begin at a suitable point mid-song in order to build to a finishing climax.

The panel may suddenly halt us in mid-piece or mid-sentence. Many players assume this means that it was unimpressed. Perhaps. We tell ourselves it means the opposite; that our capable technique, artistry and preparation are so obvious that the panel does not need to hear more. We know that auditions, exams and competitions run to tight schedules and the listeners are adept at summing up competitors' projection, tone, presentation and ability in the first few minutes.

If they halt us with brusque words, we try to stay positive and objective and not take their manner personally. Janet Delpratt, vocal professor at the Queensland Conservatorium of Music, Griffith University, says:

> Auditions are the hardest thing you will have to do. With no audience, you have to communicate to the seats or something, but you must give a performance. Whether the panel is nasty or nice, whether they grin like hyenas trying to put you at ease or sit and look dull probably doesn't make much difference. It does annoy me that the simple courtesy of introducing the contestant to the panel is, sadly, often neglected.

Unfortunately, many panellists are unaware that their manner is off-putting. Let me address those of you who serve on judging panels.

Is the player flustered because of your own abrupt manner? Would a few seconds' courtesy have revealed an exceptional, sensitive artist? Will you later hear this same player shining from a starring role or principal chair in a rival orchestra?

Think back to your formative stages. Surely, you remember your own qualms? Did the panellists' manner ever exacerbate your own nerves? Allay candidates' tensions with simple courtesies, like a few words' apology for keeping them waiting an hour or allowing them ten seconds to finish the piece rather than cutting them abruptly short.

Panellists are concerned with assessing players in a minimum of time; they want to know that players can 'deliver the goods' under pressure, for most performances involve some stress. They want to hear imagination supported by competent technique for without the latter even the most exceptional artistry would be frustrated.

Clarinetist Paul Dean says, 'Most panels are prepared to forgive the odd wrong note or slip of intonation, but are less tolerant of poor rhythm.'

John Noble, from his experience as manager of the Queensland Orchestra, advised:

Auditions – the equivalent of a job interview – are a trial for both the musicians undergoing them and for the audition panel. Unfortunately, no better method has been found to assess talent, except occasionally a trial period, if a player's background and reputation warrants. An audition can only artificially duplicate the atmosphere of a concert as the specialised listeners are there solely to judge rather than to be entertained. But if they can be entertained in the process, so much the better; they are only human after all!

On the one hand, the performer is keyed up and nervous, hoping to meet the highest standard on the day. On the other hand, the panel usually consists of hardened professionals who have heard it all before and hope that this one will be worth listening to when so many are not!

Panellists do not like to waste their valuable time. Many of them may have other things on their mind and will not be paying full attention to your work prepared so painstakingly for so many months. This is not because they don't care, rather that they have other pressures to contend with and they are frankly waiting to be impressed by what you do. Yes, panellists do want to hear a good performance, one which will make them sit up and listen. They don't want to be bored and embarrassed by your work. To the extent that you can hold their attention, you've got a chance of getting the job! They seek the best talent that they can engage and they are not concerned with your ego or belief that you should be the successful appointee. They will probably not be aware of the standard you are capable of reaching, though if their intuition suggests you could do better, they may ask you to repeat a passage or to try again at a later date.

Try again! Don't give up after a rejection or two. For eight months, Bette Midler auditioned for the same Broadway show, *Fiddler on the Roof*, every time there was a vacancy. Eventually she got a temporary place in the chorus, which gave her the advantage of knowing the production inside out when she auditioned for a star role successfully.

Conduct yourself in a professional manner. Be polite and respectful (but not fawning) towards panel members, who are usually leaders in their profession. Don't worry about feeling nervous: everyone usually is and a certain amount of nervous tension will give you that vitality and energy you need to play well. All performers worth their salt get nervous before playing.

Competitions

Bartok commented that 'competitions are for horses, not for musicians'. Musicians endure enormous physical exertion and stress on the international competition circuit. Is it worth it? The winner's exposure, recording contracts and high profile performances ensure that this provides a fast-track to a concert career. Finalists also gain from hearing their peers, from meeting people, from being heard ... but at what price?

Pianist Brenda Ogden describes her collapse from the enormous strain of the sleepless nights, the hard knot in her stomach, the suspense: 'My over-taut nerves finally snapped. Nauseous and weeping, I collapsed into bed and a doctor had to be called ... so much [was] at stake – a whole future.' (*Virtuoso: The Story of John Ogden*, Brenda Ogden & Michael Kerr, pp. 27-29)

So what can one do to diminish the strain of performing before a row of international jurors and the cream of our peers, possibly broadcast live? Pianist Carson Dron suggests: 'The most important thing is to choose repertoire which is tried and tested, which you have played many times before. Once you've done a couple of competitions, it all becomes a little easier.'

Be careful: over-practice with tense muscles in the lead-up to a competition may cause repetitive strain injury. Sydney clarinetist Deborah de Graaff discovered this, nearly slipping off her pinnacle of success:

> I had been chosen to compete in the ABC Young Artists Concerto Competition. Earlier, a too intensive practice session caused occasional twinges, the 'now and then' cramp of a too tired right thumb joint and the common neck and shoulder tension of many wind and string players. However, for one month prior to the Finals, this increased to severe pain when playing. Fearing the strain on my hands, I practised a bare hour per day. The pain was so intense that I spent the days prior to the concert with ice packs on my hand.
>
> I walked onto the stage for that Final wondering if my fingers would even respond. I won the Commonwealth Finals playing the difficult Françaix Concerto but incurred immense damage. I could not touch the instrument for some time after that.

What does one do? The prospect of winning a national or international competition makes it unthinkable to withdraw because of a sore hand! Yet to continue might jeopardise one's whole future career. In Deborah's case it nearly did so. She spent agonising years experimenting with limited playing, supports, neck straps, splints. A surgeon advised a 'cold turkey' program of total avoidance of any pain-causing activities – no playing, no cooking, no writing, no hand-sports.

Deborah returned to a successful professional career after years of patience, improving her overall fitness, correcting spinal problems through the Alexander Technique and gradually increasing her playing time. She writes: 'If anything, I love music more deeply because it was out of my reach for so long.'

Are all competitions so sobering or daunting? Is competition a bad thing in itself? During this century, competitions have increased in intensity and demand. Was there similar tension when Mozart and Clementi improvised compositions in the presence of the Emperor of Austria? Although Clementi was a gracious loser, the sharp-tongued Mozart was not a sporting victor. He jeered that Clementi played his Presto movement at a mere Moderato speed. However, he did flatter by imitation when he stole Clementi's theme for *The Magic Flute*!

Contemporaries might have thought the victory short-lived, for Mozart died in early poverty. Yet Clementi's eighty years were 'successful' enough, from child prodigy through to a high reputation as teacher, composer and piano manufacturer. We can console ourselves that what may at the time seem a clear-cut win/lose situation may later be seen in a totally improved light. Players who do not succeed in one competition may be encouraged to continue, realising that their futures may hold better results, that they may be on the brink of memorable careers.

In fact, many who have not won competitions have still gained excellent exposure as a result of competitions. When Ivo Pogorelic was passed over for the prize at the 1980 International Chopin Competition, several judges walked out, creating instant notoriety. He went on to found the world's richest piano competition, in Pasadena, making his wife head of the jury!

Are politics as rife in competitions as is rumoured? French pianist Olivier Cazal, winner of thirty international prizes, missed the main prize at the 1992 Sydney Piano Competition, but was voted People's Choice winner and was consequently offered solo tours and recording contracts. Speaking of a Tschaikovsky competition, Cazal said:

> The judges decided they needed three Russians to win the top three
> prizes because it was the 150th anniversary of the competition.
> Later, I heard that one candidate offered a bribe to jury members.
> This kind of thing happens a lot and everyone knows it …
> Competitions are a necessary evil. I don't like them, but I've
> entered more than sixty.

(Caroline Baum, 'People's Choice Wins Out', The Australian
Weekend Review, 7-8 May, 1994, p. 10)

Certainly, the international competition scene is tough. But less intense, smaller competitions are beneficial to up-and-coming artists.

Many young players respond to the challenge of an eisteddfod, where otherwise they might practise half-heartedly, with no goals in sight. The important issue is to minimise stress, to set reasonable goals and to keep a healthy perspective.

I tell my students to enter for the challenge, as I will be pleased if they play their best. If they gain a place, that's a bonus. I asked two students, each in their final year at secondary school, if they were disappointed not to gain a place. Natalie replied: 'Even if I don't do well in a competition, I still feel inspired from hearing others. I want to do better and so I work really hard until the inspiration wears off.' Andrew's reply was: 'Competitions give me a reason to perform and an opportunity to just get out and hit it straight on the head whether I win or not.'

Those disappointed by competition outcomes can be comforted by the Duc de Rochefoucauld's words: 'There are few defeats that a wise man cannot turn into victory and few victories that a fool will not turn into defeat.'

It may help to look at things from the adjudicator's perspective. It is often difficult to separate out a winner from many very good players. Imagine hearing thirty competent young children, one after the other, all playing sixteen bars of *Fairy Bells*. The poor adjudicator has about thirty seconds to hear and assess each player, write a paragraph, allocate marks and remember who played 'best' at the end of the section!

Now, there is your clue! If you wish to succeed in a competition or audition, it's important to stand out from your peers. Stun the judges with beautiful, brilliant tone that projects to the back of the hall, rather than dribbling down to the front two rows. Arrest them with the range of dynamics, tonal colour, details of articulation which state clearly, 'Have you heard such style, such imagination, such talent?' After all, the performing world is largely a matter of confidently selling yourself. With such a dynamic impression, the adjudicator may think it petty to quibble over a few mistakes.

Australian String Quartet violinist James Cuddeford puts competitions into a healthy perspective:

Competitions can be a good thing if you go in with the right attitude. I don't often compete. Some years ago, when I was a member of the Artemis Quartet, we entered an international chamber music competition in Holland. We had no pretensions to win and nothing much to lose.

Being straight after the Easter vacation, we were not out of practice, but were a little unrehearsed. In fact, in the first round or two, we were a bit disinterested, just having a nice time there with the lovely weather. Probably that was part of the reason why we won it, because we were relaxed and didn't have to justify ourselves. And having won, well, that's great, but we're still the same people.

In competitions, try to beat yourself, not others. You cannot be better than yourself at best. Above all, be a gracious loser. However disappointed you feel, keep smiling until the privacy of your car or home. Congratulate the winners – and learn from their strengths and from the situation.

Freelancing

The freelance scene has its own hazards. Remember all those stories about the understudy who stepped in at an hour's notice with a stunning performance and became famous overnight? How could we turn down a 'lucky break' and miss such prospects? The point is that the understudy had in fact learned the part. Many step in cold to situations for which they are unprepared. It's not as straightforward as it might at first appear.

Think carefully before being pressured into a short-notice gig. Are you already too busy to handle extra demands? Does it mean, as has happened to me, that you will only realise well into the first act that the borrowed bass clarinet, an instrument you play infrequently, is poorly set up and squawks abysmally? That the cues, cuts and repeats you were told are 'all written in the part' are not there, and you will go sailing off, oblivious, into a different section, wondering whether to plunge forward or back? What you thought might be a 'break' may be just that … it may break your reputation!

Clarinetist Donald Westlake gives sound advice for fledgling professionals on how and when to say 'no, thanks':

155

Imagine a scene. You have had a very busy week. Mornings you taught, afternoons you spent in the recording studio, evenings as a soloist on the Music Club circuit. Today is Saturday, a free day. After a morning in bed with a novel, an afternoon pottering in the garden, you ask your friend over for dinner. He lights the candles and uncorks the burgundy. At 6 pm, the phone rings. It is the manager of the Opera Company. 'Our first clarinetist has just fallen downstairs and broken his teeth. Curtain goes up on Rosenkavalier *in two hours. Can you come in and do the date?' Follows one of three scenarios:*

The first scenario: blind panic, together with a tremendous psychic inflation that you have been asked. You have no way of knowing you're only number six on the list, and the other five before you, recognising discretion as the better part of valour, have already refused the offer!

You know you're a duff sight-reader. You've never seen the music of Rosenkavalier. *But your ego triumphs. Despite all protestations from your friend, you rush off, leaving the dinner unserved, to arrive early and study the part. But it doesn't save you. You make countless wrong entries and drop clangers on every line. Result? The conductor, having glared at you all through the performance, snubs you in the foyer. The manager of the Opera Company crosses you off the list.*

Second scenario: You are a member of the elite when it comes to sight-reading. You have a reputation for getting everything right first time, every time. You accept the date without hesitation. You eat a relaxed dinner with your boyfriend and he drives you to the theatre in good time. You put the notes down like melted butter from beginning to end. You are invited to the post-performance supper. People talk about you for weeks afterwards. You become a legend in your time.

Third scenario: Oh, you suddenly remember! … you have an out-of-town date you couldn't possibly cancel. 'I'd loved to have done it,' you tell the manager, 'but it's just not possible this time. Please remember me next time, sir!'

You go on with your dinner as planned. Result? You may not have done anything to expand your reputation, but at least it's intact. If there's a moral to the tale it's this: know your limitations, your strengths, your weaknesses.

Confront the truth about yourself. Recognise your weaknesses. If you know you have a bad memory, why bother playing without music? If you know you're an indifferent sight-reader, don't accept dates that rely on this heavily.

Recordings

Even renowned accompanist Gerald Moore found recording sessions difficult:

> *It is all the fault of that confounded microphone; it picks up that which is imperceptible to the human ear, chronicles its evidence on tape, and is now plainly heard … The sensitive artist who does not face the microphone with awe is very exceptional. With me – and this despite my long experience – it amounts to fear.*
>
> (*Am I Too Loud?* Gerald Moore, pp.214-5)

Many, even top players, have found it harder to relax or project in recording situations because they miss the spontaneity and communication with an audience; they are less able to recapture the excitement of a live performance.

Austrian pianist and composer Artur Schnabel took years to become comfortable with recording:

> *At the concert, there is a living listener and a living performer, while, when a record is played, there is only one living being and one object which is, in a way, dead; so this contact, this 'vibration' is lost. Initially I suffered agonies and was in a state of despair each time I recorded. I felt as if I were harried to death and most unhappy. Everything was artificial – the light, the air, the sound …*
>
> (*Artur Schnabel, My Life and Music; Reflections on Music*, Colin Smythe, p. 187)

Eventually, through improvements in recording techniques and acoustic conditions and especially through working as a team with the same engineer for a decade, Schnabel became 'very pleased with the spirit of the thing'.

Guitarist Julian Bream became so uncomfortably self-conscious about recording that he took a year off:

> *The artificiality of it all had begun to drag me into despair. The quest for technical perfection and the wish to eliminate ancillary*

off-stage noises had gradually worn me down. My performances in the studio were becoming lifeless and self-conscious. My phrasing was becoming mannered and there was now a tension in my playing that said nothing about music, but plenty about my inner frustrations. So I decided to chuck it all in for the time being; I took up flying gliders instead.

(*A Life on the Road*, Julian Bream, p. 9)

Sometimes, we need the sense to temporarily back off from unnerving situations. Otherwise we may look back later and think: 'I wish I had stopped to pick more daisies.'

However, opting out seems impossible when we are trying to forge a career. Whether we perform as soloists or as part of an orchestra, recording sessions are a focal part of the performing industry.

Clarinetist Paul Dean says: 'A lot freeze up when they see the red light go on. You have to learn to play exactly the same in a recording as for an audience. It's difficult when young players are starting out, but it becomes a habit thing with experience.'

Electronic reproduction has been perfected to such a high degree that our sophisticated society expects high standards from both performers and recording technicians. We feel pressured to match the finesse of recordings in live concerts, even while realising that this perfection is an illusion.

Physical aspects may exacerbate this sense of ill-ease. Air conditioning is often unkind to singers or speakers and to instruments. If the studio is not booked immediately beforehand, it helps to arrive early to become accustomed to the atmosphere and acoustics. As the acoustics of many recording studios are particularly dry and clinical, we don't hear the reverberation of our own instruments – recording is easier in 'dry' acoustics, so such studios are usually chosen for recording pop music, with screens separating sound sources and artificial reverberation mixed in.

This 'dead' setting is necessary because of the acoustic properties of the microphones. Thus it may be difficult to hear and coordinate with colleagues. As we cannot accurately hear the balance and can barely register intonation, we must rely totally on directions from the conductor and technicians. Discipline is essential and players must be well prepared (the purpose of rehearsal is more to place microphones and balance the sound than for players to learn their parts) and alert to avoid unnecessary and expensive time on re-takes.

There are two main types of recording situations. The first involves small ensembles which overdub onto pre-recorded material. The players may feel isolated, in a vacuum separated by screens, for the studio has little 'feel'. The musicians play with machines rather than with other people and often without the security of a conductor. Because of high costs of recordings, the sponsors expect musicians to do an efficient job.

The second common situation is the larger ensemble, usually an orchestra. Here at least one has the fraternity of working with colleagues, rather than lonely minimal interaction with technicians in a glass box. It is essential to be quiet before and after recording to allow time for the reverberation.

John Noble, as both trumpeter and recording technician, could advise from both sides of the glass recording box:

Team effort achieves best results. Cooperate with the recording team as much as possible. You are in the hands of the producer, who may invite you to listen to a playback and comment on balance … if you are paying for the recording!

You need to create your own 'atmosphere' and program your state of mind by concentrating fully on the music and how you want to perform it. This will help to settle your nerves by making you less self-conscious and taking your mind off yourself and how you feel. Put yourself into a state of mind where you are determined to give of your best to the invisible audience out there. Don't allow yourself to be distracted by minor matters – think of the music and your conception of how it should sound.

If it helps, imagine playing for someone you admire, trust or love. Do anything you can which will assist in focussing your energy on the music itself. It's really a case of mind over matter.

Examinations

The preparation for examinations has been covered in detail in the author's *Practice is a Dirty Word; How to clean up your act.*

As exams and auditions are often held in a small studio, the close proximity of playing before one or two panellists may be disconcerting. Make a mistake and we'll immediately notice their pens scratching away. We must tell ourselves it is not necessarily linked to that mistake. Maybe our beautiful sound or musical phrasing triggered a flow of positive words. Realise that examiners' schedules are tight, so they must write busily throughout.

Examinations and auditions may seem more disconcerting than 'normal' concerts, largely because we miss the empathy of an audience and because possible employment is at stake. Yet we can protest too loudly about competitive or hostile atmospheres. Nerves are not actual destroyers and cannot flourish when we have the confidence of secure preparation.

Nothing comes from nothing. Yet, equally, nothing is ever wasted. A first-rate exam or audition is noticed and remembered, even if it does not secure today's goal.

Finally, examiners and panellists actually want candidates to do well and don't enjoy failing them. The examiner will give you every chance that time permits to do as well as you are able. For all circumstances – auditions, competitions, exams, recordings – security comes from the same sources: preparation well in advance. Take a deep breath, think positively, play beautifully ... and you won't need to rely on luck.

First nights

There is a mixture of emotions surrounding this long-anticipated event – breathless anticipation on the one hand, stomach-wrenching dread on the other.

Barbra Streisand was about to open with *Funny Girl* on Broadway and, as happens in most great musicals, the closer it came to opening in New York, the more tense, desperate and worried everyone became. The opening was rescheduled four times and Barbra, bearing the brunt of the show, also bore the heaviest burden: 'That's what drove me into analysis, *Funny Girl* on the stage. I was on Domitol to control my stomach. I was so frightened. I felt the pressure. Enormous pressure.'

She must have hidden her fears well as her performance was well received.

Actor Sir Laurence Olivier told a colleague:

There's a trick I've used on occasions and I find it works. Try it. Go to the theatre early on the first night and get made up well in advance of the curtain. Then, walk onto the stage and imagine that the curtain is already up and that you are facing the audience. Look out at them and shout, 'You are about to see the greatest performance of your entire theatre-going lives. And I will be giving it. You lucky people.' Tell them that once or twice, then go back to your dressing room and relax and you'll find that, when the curtain does go up, you'll have the necessary confidence.

(*The Everyman Book of Theatrical Quotes*, Donald Sinden, ed.)

Summary

- **Preparation, choice of suitable repertoire, and a positive attitude all help to ease on-the-day nerves.**

- **Where possible, check acoustics by playing in the venue beforehand.**

- **Even if our performance in a competition or audition does not win the desired result, panellists may remember us for future opportunities.**

- **Recording studios are dry and impersonal so focus on projecting the music. Preparation is essential as rehearsal is geared more for the technicians than for the musicians to learn the notes.**

Part D

The reward

11

How to love your art and let your soul soar

*Consider what your nature is able to bear before you
decide which path in life you will take.*

Epicetus

THROUGHOUT THIS BOOK, WE HAVE HEARD many voices
describe their experiences and express their feelings about
performance. They have spoken to reassure us that stage fright is
common to many, whether at the first or top rung of the ladder. Stage
fright is no respecter of persons. Each player's experience is different
and strikes in various ways.

We have learned how others have handled their various situations.
Many have found viable solutions, so that their careers and lives have
not been jeopardised.

What about those who still flounder, who have tried various angles,
but still suffer intensely from nerves? Should they drag themselves
through a career which makes their lives miserable?

To those nursing hypersensitive, tender memories of 'failed'
performances, I say, stop and consider a moment. Is the root of your
problem a need to live up to high expectations of a parent or teacher?
Now, each time you step on stage, whose approval are you still
seeking? For whom do you play? Perhaps for Grandma, who died ten
years ago? Are you still seeking parental approval, linked with the
child's basic need to be loved and protected in order to survive?
Maybe it's time you chose to play for your own enjoyment or for a
more grateful recipient of all your efforts.

Perfectionists are more likely to suffer from stage fright. This may be partly due to their natural personality, certainly, but also partly to childhood conditioning and experiences. Can any of us reach absolute perfection this side of the grave? Let us strive for excellence, rather than perfection. It is enough to do our honest best and continue to do so.

We must set ourselves reasonable goals, otherwise we find reasons to procrastinate or to give up trying. If we wait until we are perfect before competing, we will wait for ever. This sets us up for failure, depressed and frustrated because we achieve far less than our capabilities, then stall in a welter of self-judgement.

Are there reasons for stress which could be changed for the better? Perhaps you are fighting inadequate equipment? My husband's violin had often drawn compliments for the sweet tone he produced. However, when, as concertmaster of an orchestra, his solos needed more projection, his stress became intolerable, for the instrument had little carrying power. Selling that violin was a wonderful release psychologically, and he produced a similarly beautiful tone on subsequent instruments.

Perhaps the situation has become so agonising that you are physically and mentally overwhelmed, depressed by it? Take some time off and rest for a while – have a holiday or change of scene to think. Regain your perspective by spending ten minutes each day looking both inwards and also at the horizon to see the bigger picture. Discuss your qualms with an understanding teacher, counsellor, doctor, pastor or friend. Adopt a mentor who can understand and give you advice. If after such considerations the problem remains acute, seek professional help.

Is there a related field to which your expertise would be better applied? Perhaps exploring another tangent would release the tension? One violinist, after trying for years to master debilitating nerves that crippled his definite talent, realised that they were largely caused by years of high expectations and competition with his father. His musicianship has been much appreciated since he put his time and energy into conducting, teaching and administration. Trying a different angle may improve a situation. Some people would thrive in other related fields which do not require them to perform.

In our 21st century society, several changes of direction are common during a working life. How many people do you know who have stayed with the one firm all their career? A medical specialist told me wryly that he had spent thirty years climbing to the top of his ladder … only to discover it was the wrong ladder. Who knows what other exciting vistas might be seen from another ladder? The richness of life's experience may be multiplied in a totally different field.

Imagine the relief if you dumped that burden of stress! See yourself freed, a lighter, happier person. It is possible that you may be able to return to your chosen field after feeling comfortable with another tangent.

Opt out or move sideways

Some are temperamentally just not suited to a career in the spotlight. Many highly talented musicians made sensible moves away or sideways from the excess pressure of performance and were far more comfortable and productive after choosing a related form. Many 'famous names' were less 'successful' in a former guise, before discovering where their more significant skills lay. There is release and value in searching further to find the niche in which we are happier and more productive. Here, we can enjoy our art.

Why should Liszt, the great performer with all Europe at his feet, give up public performance thirty-nine years before his death? Weary of the virtuoso's lifestyle, he chose to perform only charity concerts, devoting himself to prolific composition and to inspiring others through teaching. His students idolised him and many became highly successful pianists.

In 1920, Sacheverell Sitwell described hearing Liszt and Busoni play what he described as a ghostly occasion: 'Both of them were weary, weary to death of one half of their powers, weary of the public, weary of their cheap applause, tired of stupidity.'

Singer Jenny Lind chose to leave the pressures of opera and her ecstatic audiences in favour of music that she enjoyed more:

What do you say of my having left the [opera] stage? I cannot tell you in words how happy I feel about it. I shall sing in concerts as long as I have a voice; but that only gives me pleasure ... I have begun to sing what has long been the wish of my heart – Oratorio. There, I can sing the music I love; and the words make me feel a better being.

(*Success in Music and How it is Won*, Henry T. Fink, pp. 50-51)

Camille Saint-Saëns and Cesar Franck, both prodigies, tired of the stress of early performance, found greater satisfaction playing organ and composing. Weber and Chopin were glad to avoid the platform for composition and teaching.

Put failure into perspective

We are all fallible. A few failures don't end a career. Australian pianist David Helfgott struggled back from twelve years in mental institutions to project his sheer love of music and people. Even if we sink into deep depression, into mental breakdown, we are not alone in this. Mezzosoprano Suzanne Johnston suffered such depression:

I was lost. I just gave up. I sat on a couch and ate Tim Tams ... I did not have the physical or emotional strength to deal with a role like Carmen, which takes me pretty close to my limit. I didn't want to sing any more ... I never wanted to perform in public again.

Listening to an old recording of her own singing at the age of eight brought her off the couch. 'I realised I had a gift and it was my duty to share.' She hired a personal trainer, lost seven kilograms and had her hair re-styled. 'I decided that if I was going to come back into the world, I wanted to do it looking and feeling good in my skin.' Suzanne shared her experiences because 'people find it reassuring to see someone dive into the depths and actually come out on the other side.'(Georgina Safe and Jane Albert, *Mezzo's Intermezzo, The Australian*, April 29, 2003, p. 15.]

Enjoy your art

Look around at a wide range of performances. Which players do you see actually enjoying their art? Amateurs, yes, for they are less likely to care about their reputations. They play for their own pleasure. So do jazz musicians, for they play in a more relaxed atmosphere, perhaps with a jug of beer on the piano. Improvisation allows them more autonomy and consequently more risks but there is less likelihood of boredom.

Gypsies are notorious for communicating genuine love of music. Violinist and author Kato Havas points out that the Hungarian gypsy violinists are free from nerves, able to play fiendishly difficult passages with complete ease on any violin and under any circumstances:

> *Why can they produce a tone with all the colours of the rainbow in it? Why are they able to put one through a vast range of emotional experiences at the drop of a hat? First, they are not burdened with the responsibilities of our social system. They do not have to be better than their fellows in order to succeed ... Secondly, their sole interest is the pleasure of the listeners. They are free from all obligations, except the one and only obligation to communicate.*
>
> (*Stage Fright: Its Causes and Cures*, Kato Havas, p.12)

Has our formal performance training taken a wrong direction that many now struggle to perform? Have we lost our joy, our love of our art? Are we too busy striving for technical perfection, for faultless memorisation, to communicate warmth and vitality? If this is so, I urge us all – teachers, institutions, parents, performers and audiences – to encourage all that is positive, resisting the temptation to carp about minor faults. Look beneath the surface of technical facility for the deep meanings of soul and spirit below, both in the composition and in the performer's interpretation.

Channel weakness into strength

As we face seemingly unsurmountable tensions and fears before an audience, it may be heartening to know that others have turned such 'weaknesses' into strengths, into whole careers. Take Enrico Caruso, the incomparable tenor. He acknowledged that the unique quality of his voice was a product of stage fright!

> *The consciousness that absolutely unprecedented things are expected of me makes me ill and I fail to do half as well as I might do otherwise. I am seized with nervousness and the anguish alone makes my voice what it is. There is no personal merit in it ... Everything is the fault of that redoubtable deity called* le trac

(stage fright). And apparently my fright increases from day to day, for people say to me regularly: 'You have never sung so well as today.'

(*Success in Music and How it is Won*, Henry T. Fink, pp. 210-211)

Keep your perspective and sense of humour

As performance problems affect the whole person, it is easy to become hypersensitive and to take ourselves too seriously. Ask yourself: Will this matter in four days' time? In four weeks? Four months? Four years? An ability to see the funny side of a situation and to laugh off embarrassing incidents is a great asset. Cultivate this.

Humour is a powerful weapon to combat stress. Laughter has been shown to reduce pain, possibly because it activates the release of endorphins – hormones similar to morphine. These are produced naturally by the body to inhibit both the physical mechanisms of pain and our emotional response to it.

Face the music

At whatever level of involvement we choose, we must accept the responsibility for our performance. Many performers advise that the most obvious, foolproof safeguard to avoid nerves is thorough preparation well before the event. Composer Nicholas Rimsky-Korsakov noted that stage fright is in inverse proportion to the degree of preparation.

With the conviction that comes from honest work, with solid preparation, and with the centring and calming of meditation or prayer, we can hold up our heads and do our best. If we know that we have these secure foundations beneath us, we can accept any failings without unnecessary self-flagellation. Eleanor Roosevelt said: 'No-one can make you feel inferior without your consent.'

Our next challenge will be to face success. Many talented people may focus on negatives through subconscious self-sabotage, as a stalling tactic to avoid the responsibilities that come with achievement. This is beautifully expressed by Marianne Williamson, in her book *A Return to Love:*

Our deepest fear is
not that we are inadequate.
Our deepest fear is
that we are powerful beyond measure.
It is our light, not our darkness,
that most frightens us.
We ask ourselves,
'Who am I to be brilliant, gorgeous,
talented and fabulous?'
Actually, who are you not to be? You are a child of God.
Your playing small doesn't serve the world.
There's nothing enlightened about
shrinking so that other people
won't feel insecure around you.
We were born to make manifest
the glory of God that is within us.
It is not just in some of us; it's in everyone.
And as we let our own light shine,
we unconsciously give to other people
permission to do the same.
As we are liberated from our own fear,
our presence automatically liberates others.

Art does not consist of technique alone. We performers must enrich our own spirits in order to communicate the composer's or writer's inner thoughts. This requires exploration of our deeper souls, our meanings. Some down-time, recreation and breathing space are essential to renew creativity. Be kind to yourself. Allow yourself to be fallible, human.

Set yourself reasonable goals within your capabilities, but allow space to grow. Life is a journey and so is the maturing of our talent. Above all, don't cripple yourself with unrealistic perfectionist expectations. Instead, be grateful for your opportunities to share in the depth, beauty and spirit of great music. Revel in these.

Free the sheer enjoyment of performing. Let your spirit soar!

The performing arts – music, theatre, dance – offer a rich life, and also a vital therapy, brimming as they do with such beauty, expressing the vast range of emotions we may feel in a lifetime. Certainly, technical effort is needed to attain their heights, but this must never be at the expense of the awareness of their beauty, warmth, excitement and passion.

Give this to others. Love your art, send this love out past the footlights to your listeners and they will respond, appreciate and enjoy. Your fears will be put to flight. Play beautifully. Enjoy!

Bibliography

Apthorp, Shirley, 'Touching Triumph on the World Stage', *The Australian*, June 14, 1996, p. 11.

Baum, Caroline, 'People's Choice Wins Out', *The Australian*, Weekend Review, 7-8 May, 1994, p. 10.

Bergan, Ronald, *Dustin Hoffman*, Virgin, 1991

Campbell, Margaret, 'Lynn Harrell: Principal Values', *The Strad*, August 1984.

Dennison, Paul E. and Gail E., *Brain Gym: Teacher's Edition*, Edu-Kinesthetics, Ventura, 1989.

Duval, David, *The World of the Concert Pianist*, Victor Gollancz, 1985.

Elder, Dean, *Pianists at Play*, The Instrumentalist Co, 1982.

Evans, Andrew, *The Secrets of Musical Confidence: How to Maximise Your Performance Potential*, HarperCollins, 1994.

Evans, Andrew, 'Fear and Trembling', *Music Teacher*, May 1994.

Fink, Henry T., *Success in Music and How It is Won*, Charles Schribner, 1909.

Flesch, Carl, *The Art of Violin Playing*, Carl Fischer, 1924.

Fonteyn, Margot, *Autobiography*, Hamish Hamilton, 1975.

Gelatt, Roland, *Music Makers: Some Outstanding Musical Performers of our Day,* Da Capo Press, 1972.

Gelb, Michael, *Present Yourself*, Aurum Press, 1988.

Havas, Kato, *Stage Fright: Its Causes and Cures, with Special Reference to the Violin*, Bosworth, 1976.

Kahn, Albert E., *Joys and Sorrows – Pablo Casals*, Eel Pie Publishing, 1970.

Farkas, Philip, *The Art of French Horn Playing*, Summy-Birchard, 1956.

Kennedy, Nigel, *Always Playing*, Weidenfeld and Nicholson, 1991.

Kirk, H.L., *Pablo Casals: A Biography*, Hutchinson and Co., 1994.

Lim, Anne, 'Playing for Keeps', *The Australian*, Weekend Review, April 23-24, 1994, p. 10.

Litson, Jo., 'Risky Business', *The Australian*, Weekend Review, October 23-24, 1996, p. 10.

Mair, George, *Bette: An Intimate Biography of Bette Midler*, Aurum Press, 1995.

Matheopoulos, Helena, *Diva: The New Generation: The Sopranos and Mezzos of the Decade Discuss their Roles,* Little, Brown and Co., 1998.

Maychick, Diana, *Meryl Streep: The Reluctant Superstar,* Robson Books, 1984.

McCallion, Michael, *The Voice Book*, Faber, 1988.

Menuhin, Yehudi, *Unfinished Journey*, Futura Publications, 1976.

Moore, Gerald, *Am I Too Loud?* Penguin, 1962.

Netter, Susan, *Paul Newman and Joanne Woodward* Piatkus, 1989.

Neuhaus, Heinrich, *The Art of Piano Playing*, Barrie and Jenkins, 1973.

Newman, Ernest, *The Man Liszt*, Victor Gollancz, 1970.

Nelson, Robert B., *Louder and Funnier: A Practical Guide for Overcoming Stagefright in Speechmaking*, Ten Speed Press, 1988.

Ogden, Brenda Lucas and Kerr, Michael, *Virtuoso: The Story of John Ogden*, Hamish Hamilton, 1981.

Palmer, Tony, *Julian Bream: A Life on the Road*, MacDonald, 1982.

Parker, John, *Michael Douglas: Acting on Instinct*, Headline, 1995.

Pavarotti, Luciano, with Wright, William, *My Own Story*, Sidgwick and Jackson, 1981.

Roth, Henry, *Great Violinists in Performance*, Panjandrum Books, 1987.

Secrest, Meryle, *Leonard Bernstein, A Life*, Alfred A. Knopf, 1994.

Riistad, Eloise, *A Soprano on Her Head*, Real People Press, 1982.

Salmon, Paul, and Meyer, Robert G., *Notes from the Green Room*, Lexington, 1992.

Schnabel, Artur, *My Life and Music; Reflections on Music*, Colin Smythe, 1970.

Schonberg, Harold C., *The Great Pianists*, Simon and Schuster, 1963.

Secrest, Meryle, *Leonard Bernstein*, Alfred A. Knopf, 1994.

Sitwell, Sacheverell, *Liszt*, Dover, 1967.

Shand, John, 'All Good Fun: The Life and Times of James Morrison', *Australasian Jazz'n'Blues*, Volume 2, No.4, 1995.

Sinden, Donald (ed.), *The Everyman Book of Theatrical Quotes,* J.M. Dent, 1987.

Spohr, Louis, *Autobiography*, Da Capo Press, 1969.

Stein, Keith, 'Overcoming Tension in Playing', *The Clarinet*, Spring 1979.

Spada, James, *Streisand: The Woman and the Legend*, W.H. Allen, 1982.

Walker, Alan (ed.), *Robert Schumann: The Man and His Music,* Barrie and Jenkins, 1971.

Wagar, Jeannine, *Conductors in Conversation, G.K. Hall, 1991.*

Williamson, Marianne, *A Return to Love,* HarperCollins, 1992, 1996.

Index

175

Here are the tools to

Star Performance!

Workshops & books
by Ruth Bonetti
enable confident performance

Practice is a Dirty Word - Rescues teachers, parents and students from the bogey of practice. Helps developing musicians to "work smart" so they can enjoy their playing and realise their potential. ISBN: 0 9578861 5 2

> "I strongly recommend the book for anyone, especially those for whom the fun has disappeared from 'playing' music."
>
> Jeffrey Scott Doebler, Ph.D.,
> Director of Music Education and Bands, Valparaiso University, Indiana, USA
> President, Indiana Music Educators Association,USA

> "For any parent or teacher who has come close to tearing their hair out over their child's music practice, this book is a godsend! Can you imagine never again having to nag your student to practice? Ruth Bonetti's book could be the end of all your woes!"
>
> Mary Nemet, Australian Music Teacher

Confident Music Performance - You've practised hard, you have ability – but are you able to walk on stage and shine? This book will help you face the audience without fear, enjoy the moment and succeed.

Shows how to:
• Cure shakes, jitters, brain fog
• Excel in exams, auditions, concerts
• Survive mistakes and hazards on stage
• Enjoy confident performance   ISBN: 0 9578861 6 0

> "This easy to read gem of a book gives lots of practical, down- to-earth advice. Regardless of what instrument you play, this is a valuable asset for both teachers and performers. Written in a sympathetic, user-friendly style, is highly recommended. "
>
> Dr. Rita Crew, The Studio Magazine

Don't Freak Out - Speak Out - Public Speaking With Confidence. Invaluable guide - Covers all aspects of preparation - mental, emotional, physical and presentation. A must for all who stand up and speak in public. ISBN 0 9578861 0 1

Available also as audio CD and e-book at **www.ruthbonetti.com**

What critics and readers say about Ruth Bonetti's books...

What a life-saver! Your book really helped me get over my stage-fright.

Anna Laino, Ohio, USA (singer)

.....so helpful and inspiring that I am now incorporating your principles into my performing and teaching - truly a needed resource in this day of beta blockers and high pressure audition situations. I know of no other book that addresses this issue in such an engaging manner. It is essential equipment for any musician, professional or student.

Mary Natvig, Ph.D, Associate Professor, Bowling Green
State University, Ohio, USA

Written in good, everyday English and easy to read, even for a person with another native language. I am happy to recommend it for 'external use' to prevent 'internal abuse.'

Carl Friedner, music journalist, Swedish Radio, Stockholm

As a performer who has read everything I can find which deals with issues affecting performance, I find this book more useful to me on a daily basis than most I have read. You attack the subjects of panic-like states of nervousness head-on with helpful and very specific advice.

David Oyen, D.M.A, Assistant Professor of Bassoon and Theory,
Morehead State University, Kentucky, USA

Most absorbing and illuminating reading. Ruth Bonetti's enthusiasm and genuine care infects every page. All this positive and practical advice can only help us to become happier and more contented human beings!

Regis Danillon, *Bravura*,

Ruth Bonetti's Workshops create
Performance Confidence

Ruth's seminars cover the gamut from positive preparation to confident performance. Her practical solutions empower both teachers and students to realise their potential, to project with poise, clarity and confidence.

Help Students Practise for Success –
and Ensure STAR PERFORMANCE!

"Have you practised at all this week?"

Many teachers and parents, are disheartened by students who make excuses, give up – or when talented, conscientious musicians lose confidence in performance and don't realise their potential.

Learn:

• Constructive strategies to motivate and inspire students' practice
• How to empower students to perform to their ability
• Practical techniques enable you to assert your voice in classrooms, rehearsals and parent-teacher meetings

Sessions are available as a one-day seminar or choose individual modules.

You can choose from:

• Day, half-day and one-hour interactive workshops/presentations
• One-on-one workshops and master classes

Also by Ruth Bonetti - available at leading music stores:

Enjoy Playing the Clarinet (Oxford University Press)
— A comprehensive beginner tutor (listed, AMEB Grades 1-4)

Clarinet: Series 2, Australian Music Examinations Board syllabus books Grades 1-4 — selected and edited by Ruth Bonetti

---

WORKSHOPS FOR MUSIC TEACHERS

Topics include:

- How to Motivate, Retain and Inspire Students
- Professional Parent-Teacher Communication
- Prepare Students for Confident Performance
- Empower Students to Realise Performance Potential

WORKSHOPS / MASTER CLASSES FOR STUDENTS

Include:

- Confident Oral Presentations
- How to Practise for Success
- How to Impress the Examiner – and Excel
- Scales and Arpeggios Demystified
- 7 Easy Habits for Confident Performance
- Enjoy Playing the Clarinet

Days of Excellence Program (Choose modules to suit your program)

TALK FOR PARENTS

- Help your Child Excel with Music

From her perspective as an AMEB examiner, educator and mother of three sons, Ruth solves common issues such as:

"How can I enforce boring practice?"

"Should I sit in on lessons?"

"How to ease performance stress?"

"My child has talent but has lost interest! How do I rekindle their enjoyment?"

Bookings and Info:

www.ruthbonetti.com

ruth@ruthbonetti.com

Ph. (61 7) 3300 2286 or 0411 782 404

Fax: (61 7) 3300 5786

Ruth Bonetti has presented student and faculty seminars extensively in universities and schools across Australia, in Europe and in America, where her seminars were repeated by popular demand:

"Ruth Bonetti was a faculty asset far beyond our expectations. Students responded so positively to her coaching and vibrant personality that we had to expand her workload and schedule additional sessions. I cannot say enough positive about Mrs Bonetti's work as a performance coach."

Dr Victor E. Gebauer, Executive Director,
Lutheran Music Program, Minneapolis,USA

After adjunct teaching in Sweden, France, Germany and England, Ruth taught clarinet and pedagogy at the Conservatorium of Music, Griffith University for 15 years and has experience teaching students of all ages and levels. She travels extensively giving keynote and seminar presentations to empower teachers and students for confident performance.

"Ruth delighted the participants with her infectious good humour and vibrant personality. Her presentations were a highlight due to Ruth's ability to involve everyone, her enthusiasm and charisma."

Malcolm F. Potter, President,
Music Teachers' Assocn.,South Australia

"A healing, compassionate little book."

Marjery Smith, Lecturer, University of Newcastle

"I like your relaxed writing style and all the practical natural remedies you suggest. It really is a book for the 21st century!"

Margaret Brandman, composer and teacher

ORDER FORM

Ruth's Ezines - Subscribe at www.ruthbonetti.com
- *Music Educators' Energise* - FREE
- *Crisp Confidence* (for presenters) - FREE
- *Performance Power* - FREE
- *MusoMotivator Weekly ezine* (Annual Subscription $50)

Books by Ruth Bonetti

Please send me:

_____ copies of *Confident Music Performance* $25

_____ copies of *Don't Freak Out - Speak Out* Book $20
             CD $26 E-book $25

_____ copies of *Practice is a Dirty Word* $20

_____ copies of *Special Pack;* buy all 3 books ($55 - save $10)

        Post & Pack $3 per item. Prices include GST.
        Cheques Payable to "Musica Bonetti" (ABN: 54 569 725 734)
        PO Box 422, The Gap Qld 4061 Australia

Name:_____

Address:_____

State:_____Postcode/zip:_____Country: _____

Phone: _____Email: _____

Credit Card orders online at www.ruthbonetti.com

For discounts on bulk orders and class sets contact:
Ph: (617) 3300 2286   Mobile: 0411 782 404
Fax: (617) 3300 5786   Email: ruth@ruthbonetti.com